Front-Line
Thames

Michael Foley

The History Press

First published in the United Kingdom in 2008 by
The History Press
The Mill • Brimscombe Port • Stroud • Gloucestershire • GL5 2QG

Reprinted 2009

British Library Cataloguing in Publication Data
A catalogue record for this book is available from the British Library.

ISBN 978-07509-5050-3

To Beacon Hill School, South Ockendon, Essex
A special place for special children,
where happiness and achievement go hand in hand

All images are from the author's personal collection unless otherwise stated.

Title page illustration: An old map of the Thames from Vauxhall Bridge to
Southwark Bridge.

Typeset in 10.5/13pt Sabon
Typesetting and origination by
The History Press.
Printed and bound in Malta.

Contents

Introduction & Acknowledgements

There are times in your life when you read a statement and you wish you had said it first. That was exactly what I thought when I read the following by the British politician, John Burns: 'The Thames is liquid history.' I had already realised this fact while writing previous books about Kent and Essex, two of the counties that border the river as it reaches the sea. Both of these books included details of several defensive structures either on the banks of, or close to the Thames.

The river has played such an important part in the history of the country and it was the defence of the river, especially between the tower and the sea, which first caught my imagination. However, there is so much more to the river than just the part below London. The majority of the conflicts throughout history that were enacted close to or on the river actually occurred above London. Hopefully, this book will inform some who, like me previously, thought that the Thames above the capital had always been a peaceful, serene place.

Unlike my previous 'Front-Line' books, which were arranged alphabetically, *Front-Line Thames* is compiled in the order of progression from the sea to the source.

I would like to thank Richard Milligan for reading the manuscript and for his help and suggestions and Frank Turner for allowing me to use his illustrations.

Although every attempt has been made to find the copyright owners of all the illustrations, anyone whose copyright has been unintentionally breached should contact the author through the publisher.

Michael Foley, 2008

ONE

Before the Normans

The upper reaches of the Thames may seem a quiet, rural place now. It is as the river gets closer to the sea that we think of the great defensive structures and defence against the invader. In the days before the Norman Conquest, however, the river in the Thames Valley marked the border between the territories of a number of early British tribes. In later Saxon times, the Thames marked the border between the kingdoms of Mercia, to the north of the river, and Wessex to the South.

The Thames Valley was also the site of numerous early defensive structures. The river was narrower in this area and thus easier to cross, which meant that armies

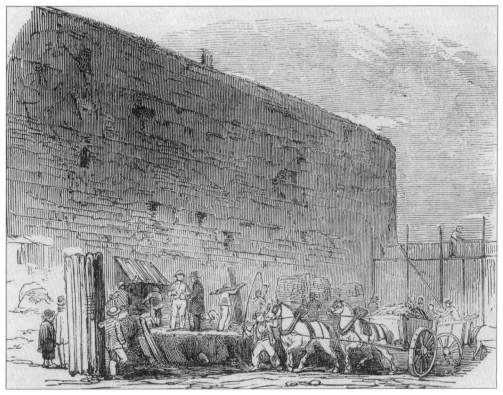

The remains of the Roman Wall at Tower Hill are thought to be the only remnants of the Roman defences in London. During the nineteenth century there were plans to demolish it, which were thankfully abandoned.

travelling from north to south chose sites above London to cross; this led to the creation of these sites to defend river crossings.

The source of many of the early defensive structures are often not clear. Although they may originally date from the Bronze Age, they have often been re-used by later settling groups such as the Roman and Vikings, which often cloud their origins. The same could be said of the sites of battles, whose positions are often disputed.

The landing points of the Roman invasions have never been proved beyond doubt. There seems to a partial agreement that during the Claudian invasion there was a battle near the Medway before the Roman army stopped at some point on the Thames to await the arrival of Emperor Claudius. Where this may have been is also a matter of some conjecture.

Another lesser-known Roman invasion took place in the third century when Carausius declared himself Emperor of Britain, which led to even more dispute. The invasion led by Constantius to re-take Britain for Rome from Carausius's killer and usurper, Allectus, took part in two separate forces. Where they landed was the basis for another dispute – one view is that the force led by Constantius actually sailed up the Thames to London.

This invasion has also led to another theory: some writers believe that the Saxon shore forts such as the one at Reculver may have been built to stop this invasion by Rome, rather than the commonly held belief that they were constructed to stop later raids by Saxons.

THANET

The Isle of Thanet played a major part in the settlement of early Kent by invaders from the continent. In 449 AD, King Vortigern asked Jutish leaders Hengist and Horsa for help against Pictish raiders. Although the Jutes originally arrived in a few ships, more of them came later and settled on Thanet. Within ten years, they had become more of a threat than an amenable ally – they eventually conquered most of Kent.

Thanet also became a Viking stronghold and the Norsemen wintered there in 851 AD. Over 300 ships anchored on the Isle's coastline at one point; it was from here that they attacked Canterbury, defeating Beorhtwulf, King of Mercia.

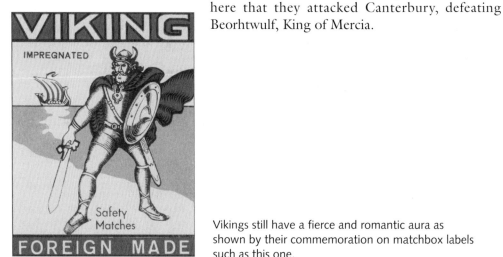

Vikings still have a fierce and romantic aura as shown by their commemoration on matchbox labels such as this one.

Materials from the old Roman fort were used to build the church at Reculver, which has since disappeared owing to subsidence. The church towers were left as an aid to shipping and parts of the fort also remain.

RECULVER

The area around Reculver was probably occupied before the Romans arrived. It is believed that the Roman defences there began life as a signal station. The settlement developed into fortified barracks before becoming a fort. Its original purpose may well have been to defend the entrance to the Thames.

Reculver developed into the site of a Roman square fort, with 10ft-thick walls and round corners. There were no known bastions, although one gate was known to be in the west wall, as well as a ditch that surrounded the fortifications. The site covered around 7½ acres. It is believed by some to have been one of the Saxon Shore Forts. These were supposedly built to stop Saxon raiders as the Roman rule of Britain drew to a close.

A town grew up around the fort, which was generally in keeping with Roman military stations. The inhabitants of the town would have made their living providing services and goods for the soldiers in the fort.

During the Saxon period, King Ethelbert gave up his home in Canterbury to Augustine and built a new palace at Reculver. A monastery was also built on the site in the seventh century, using materials from the disused fort. This was abandoned once raids by Vikings made its continued existence too dangerous.

SHOEBURYNESS

It has been a long-held belief that the site of an ancient camp at Shoeburyness was in fact of Viking provenance. More recent excavations, however, have shown it was actually of Iron Age origin. The camp could well have been used by the Vikings at a much later date.

There is no doubt that there was a Viking camp at Shoebury, which was mentioned in the *Anglo Saxon Chronicle*. When the Viking camp at Benfleet was attacked by King Alfred, the surviving Vikings moved to Shoebury. The actual name of Shoebury is thought to be based on this horseshoe-shaped Viking camp. 'Burh' was the name for a fortified place and 'sceo' was shoe, which in this case meant horseshoe. Shoeburyness has another connection with the later barracks in the area, which were called Horseshoe Barracks.

MEDWAY

The sites of Roman invasions and the battles that took place during the conquests are always open to debate. One view of an event during the Claudian invasion of 43 AD is that a Roman army of 40,000 men under General Auluslatius fought a two-day battle against the Catuvellauni tribe somewhere close to the Medway. This could have been south of Rochester.

The Catuvellauni tribe were dominant in the south-east of the country and their capital was Colchester in Essex. The defeated Britons from the Medway battle are believed to have retreated across the Thames. The victorious Roman army supposedly waited somewhere on the Thames for the Emperor Claudius to arrive before moving on to Colchester. The Romans then took Colchester using elephants, which would have been a fearful sight for the defenders of the town, who had, no doubt, never seen such animals.

PRITTLEWELL

The remains of another ancient camp are to be found at Prittlewell. It is close to the head of the River Roach and is about 800ft by 650ft. The defences consisted of a rampart and a ditch. It seems to have been an early hill fort, which would make it one of the earliest of the Thames defences. The area around Southend seems to have been well defended from the earliest times; recent archaeological finds show that it was also an important site in Saxon times.

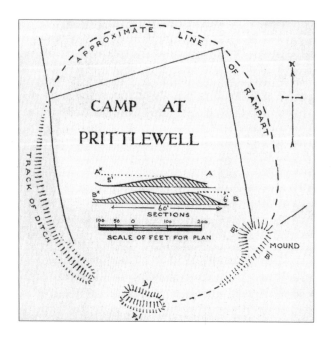

The camp at Prittlewell was an early hill fort. These forts were often used in times of crisis and not permanently manned.

BENFLEET

There was another fortified camp at Benfleet, which in 894 AD was occupied by Haesten and a large Viking army. According to the *Anglo Saxon Chronicle*, Benfleet was attacked by King Alfred's forces, who completely routed the Vikings. They destroyed the Viking ships and took the contents of the camp, including women and children, to London. When the nineteenth-century railway was being built in the area, a large number of burnt ships and human skeletons were found which are thought to originate from this battle.

MUCKING

It is interesting that a book covering the history of Essex, *Forgotten Thameside* written in 1951, makes no mention of Anglo Saxon or Roman finds in Mucking but extensive excavations thereafter found evidence of large settlement of the area. Mucking was the site of an Iron Age fort, which overlooked the Thames. Hill forts in the Iron Age are believed to have been places of occasional refuge in times of conflict, rather than permanent defensive settlements, and this fort may have been used by the local farming population.

There are also signs of Roman occupation in the area, in an agricultural rather than a defensive setting. It can be safely assumed that a period of uncertainty and lack of organised government followed in the time after the Romans left. It is argued by some that Mucking may have been one of the first organised areas of defence used by the Saxons against any further invaders.

A rather romantic view of a Roman soldier from an old print with Roman ships passing in the background. The tower to the left looks more medieval than Roman, however.

RAINHAM

Rainham is close to Mucking and also had a small Iron Age enclosure dating between 50 BC and 50 AD. It had triple ditches and banks and was about 256ft by 276ft. There was an earthen rampart with a wooden palisade. Its small size must mean that it was a defendable refuge.

There were also several later Saxon finds in the area, including a very rare glass drinking horn now in the British Museum.

BARKING

The River Roding flows into the Thames at Barking and was once an important means of travel. There was an ancient Hill Fort by the Roding at Uphall. Although the site may have been from the Bronze Age, it was also used during the Iron Age. Barking is believed to have Roman connections and Roman ships may have sailed up the Roding to Uphall. The strong defensive position of the fort has also led to the belief that it may have been used by Vikings as well.

The abbey at Barking was one of the richest in the area and was attacked by the Vikings in 870 AD. This resulted in the massacre of its inhabitants, the theft of the Abbey's treasures and the burning of the buildings. It led to a gap of around a century before the abbey was rebuilt during a lull in attacks by the Vikings.

GREENWICH

Although Greenwich was close to the route of the Roman road of Watling Street, no evidence of a large Roman settlement has been found there. There have been a number of Saxon burials found in the area, dating from around the seventh century.

One group that did spend time at Greenwich, and used it as a defended base, were the Vikings. In 1012 they wintered in the area and used it as a base to raid Canterbury, where they slaughtered many of the town's inhabitants. They took Aelfheah, the archbishop, hostage but, when they were unable to get a ransom, they killed him during a drunken feast.

Although the sight of longboats may have struck terror into the people at the time, they are now nothing more than a romantic form of illustration for a matchbox.

RIVER LEA

A strong Viking force was camped on the River Lea when King Alfred supposedly changed the course of the river to stop the Vikings from using their ships; they then fled overland. It is thought that there may be some truth behind this legend; Alfred may have actually reopened a silted-up channel of the river, which made the water level drop and prevented the Vikings from sailing further upriver.

LONDON

Despite the theories of some academics, it is unlikely that a pre-Roman town existed where London is now situated. Those who do believe that a Celtic village or fort preceded the Roman town believe it was called Lynn-Din. It is not even clear if this was where, as is often argued, Julius Caesar first crossed the Thames. It is thought, however, that the Romans built a bridge across the river somewhere in the vicinity of London quite early in their occupation.

There seems to have been a Roman settlement on the south bank of the river. It was described by Tacitus as a place of merchants. This could have been a civilian settlement near Southwark, while a military fort stood on the north bank; this is

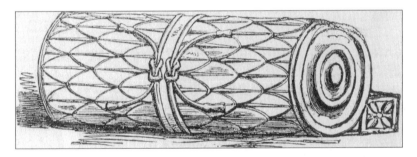

Part of a sarcophagus found at Tower Hill in the nineteenth century.

The Roman Wall at Tower Hill is the lower part of this structure. The medieval wall was built on top.

proven by the remains of the wall that surrounded it. Ptolemy described London as a city of Kent, so this seems to bear that out.

There are remains of the Roman wall at Tower Hill. In the mid-nineteenth century, there were plans to pull the wall down but, thankfully, this was stopped. It is thought to be the only remains of the Roman wall in London, although only the lower part is Roman. The medieval wall was later built on top of it.

Stones from a Roman building were also found at Tower Hill when the base of the wall was discovered during excavations in 1852. This discovery included part of a sarcophagus found by a workman tapping his foot against it while eating his dinner. This had an inscription cut into it.

A statue of a Roman at Tower Hill, thought to be the Emperor Trajan.

When County Hall was being built in 1910, the remains of a Roman ship were found, dating from around the end of the third century. Although built in the Roman style, the material used was timber from the south of England.

After the Romans left, there is some doubt about how important London was. The Saxons did not have much use for towns, but there must have been a native population; it was much later that London became an important Saxon town.

When the Vikings began to raid the country in the ninth century, they often sailed up the Thames to attack settlements and abbeys both north and south of the Thames. They attacked London itself in 839 AD. In the late ninth century, the Vikings wintered on the Thames close to London where they killed the Archbishop of Canterbury who they had taken hostage. The Vikings occupied London itself from 872 AD. When Alfred defeated the Vikings in 886 AD, he began to use the old walled town as a defensive position. It is believed to be from this point that London became the centre of much of what happened in England.

In 994 AD, Swein attacked London with ninety-four ships but was driven off. He returned in 1013 and drove King Ethelred away. Swein died the following year and his son Canute became king. He was then driven out of London by the vengeful Ethelred but returned with 340 ships. Canute supposedly dug a channel and pulled his ships round London Bridge. They were again driven off but, after a battle at Ashingdon in Essex, Canute was victorious and reclaimed the throne.

The Godwin family were later to become one of the most powerful families in the country until they fell out with King Edward the Confessor, lost their lands and were banished. In 1052, the Godwins returned in force and sailed unopposed up the Thames to London. When they landed at Southwark they were cheered by the population. Edward's army faced them from the northern bank of the river. The

A plaque mounted on a wall at Tower Hill which is a copy of an inscribed stone found there in the nineteenth century.

Bishop of Winchester eventually mediated and Godwin was given his lands back after swearing allegiance to the king. They were reunited with Edward, and Harold Godwin became king after Edward's death.

BRENTFORD

Brentford is one of many sites where it was claimed that Julius Caesar crossed the Thames. This was to attack Cassivellanus at Verulam. Later armies also used the ford to cross the river here.

In 1016, Edmund Ironside gathered a large army and crossed the Thames at Brentford to defeat the Danes there. He crossed the Thames by the ford and defeated their army on the south bank. Large numbers of the king's men were drowned when they went in front of the army trying to seize loot. It also seems that Edmund crossed the river at Brentford several times in pursuit of the Vikings.

KINGSTON UPON THAMES

A number of Roman camps have been discovered in the area of Kingston. Sometimes the description of a camp can be misleading for the Romans normally created earthworks and a ditch around their camps, even if they were only there for one night. A camp may, therefore, be nothing more than a one-night stop over.

In 838 AD, Kingston was the site of the Witan of King Egbert and supposedly the site of the coronation of seven Saxon kings, who used the coronation stone, which

A drawing of the King's Stone used during the coronations of seven Saxon kings at Kingston-upon-Thames.

Below: The position of the King's Stone in Kingston in the early twentieth century.

is now placed near the Guildhall. The seven kings crowned there were: Edward the Elder in 899 AD; Athelstan in 924 AD; Edmund I in 939 AD; Edred in 946 AD; Edwy in 955 AD; Edward the Martyr in 975 AD and Ethelred II in 979 AD. Kings in those days obviously did not last very long . . . .

CHERTSEY

There was a Benedictine abbey at Chertsey founded by Erkenwald, the Bishop of London, in 666 AD, and it had strong connections with the one at Barking. Both were founded by Erkenwald and, while he was the abbot at Chertsey, his sister was in charge at Barking. Both abbeys were destroyed by the Vikings.

Chertsey was destroyed in 869 AD when Abbot Beocca and nearly a hundred priests were slaughtered. The abbey was re-founded by King Edgar in 964 AD.

READING

Reading featured in the conflict between the Vikings and the Saxons on a number of occasions. The Danes made a base there in 871 AD for their campaign against Wessex. There was a battle between an ealdorman named Aethelwulf and the Vikings, which Aethelwulf won. A few days later, King Ethelred and his brother Alfred led a large army to Reading. There was a long battle during which Aethelwulf was killed. It seems that the Vikings were undefeated because the following year they went from Reading to London. In 1006, a Viking army returned to Reading to undertake yet more raiding.

Viking warriors making ready to attack land-based defences.

Streatley Hill overlooks the Thames where it was once the border between the Saxon kingdoms of Wessex and Mercia.

WALLINGFORD

Although thought to have Roman origins, the town of Wallingford is believed to have later become a fortified Saxon town. It also played its part in the battle against the Vikings. In 1006, an army of Danes, who had wintered on the Isle of Wight, attacked Wallingford and, in the words of the *Anglo Saxon Chronicle*, 'scorched it all up.'

In 1013, Swein's army attacked London but, after being driven off, came to Wallingford to cross the Thames on their way to Bath.

DORCHESTER

Dorchester was the site of large Iron Age earthworks on Sinodun Hill, which showed its strategic position. This was capitalised on by the Romans and Dorchester became a Roman town. There are other old defensive works, such as Dyke Hills, which may have been Roman, that were made to face the British fortifications. There was also thought to have been a channel linking the Thames and the Thame as an extra defensive ditch.

Dyke Hills, Dorchester, are the remains of old defensive earthworks, believed by some to be of Roman origin, which were built to oppose nearby British defences.

THE WITTENHAMS

There are two Wittenham villages, Long and Little, about a mile apart. There was a nearby Iron Age fort on Castle Hill. Celtic, Saxon and Roman graves and artefacts have been found in the area. This included an Iron Age sword and scabbard found close to Day's Lock. It was thought that the fort was an Atrebates stronghold, where they fought against the invasion of Julius Caesar. This may not have been quite accurate, but no other definite answer as to its origins are in place. The fort may have later been used by the Romans.

Day's Lock was the site of a find of an Iron Age sword.

Wittenham was the site of an Iron Age fort, which is believed to have been an Atrebates stronghold from where they fought the Romans under Caesar.

ABINGDON

A large Iron Age defensive structure was discovered in Abingdon in the 1990s. It had a number of defensive ditches and used the Thames and its tributary, the Ock, as defensive barriers. It was also used during the Roman period.

KEMPSFORD

Kempsford was supposedly the site of a Saxon palace. In 800 AD, Ethelmund, Ealdorman of the Wiceii, crossed the river there and attacked Weohstan of the Wilsceti – both men were killed. The Wilsceti from Wiltshire seemed to have been victorious. Some relics, perhaps from the battle between the Saxon armies, were found in the area in 1670.

CRICKLADE

The river at Cricklade is quite narrow but nevertheless it was an important barrier as it was the frontier of Wessex during Saxon times. It was often used as the crossing point for numerous armies on their way to battle. King Alfred supposedly crossed the river here when going to fight the vikings. Ethelwold crossed the river there in 905 after a raid into neighbouring Mercia and Canute also crossed the river at Cricklade in 1016 on a mission to burn and loot Warwickshire. There was thought to have been a Saxon burgh in the area to defend the river which would seem to be a reasonable assumption owing to its use as a river crossing and as the Vikings seem to have been regular visitors to the area.

When Canute crossed the river there it was recorded in the Anglo-Saxon Chronicle that he was accompanied by 160 ships. Due to the shallow state of the river at this point it would seem that large fleets of ships were unlikely to have been able to sail this far up river. One explanation of this could be that armies in those times were measured in the size of ships crews which would have been less than a hundred men. Canute's army may then have been the size of 160 ships crews although the ships probably did not accompany them.

CIRENCESTER

Cirencester was the old Roman town of Corinium, which stood at the junction of several Roman roads. It was also the site of a number of battles. According to the *Anglo Saxon Chronicle*, in 577 AD, Cathwine and Ceawlin fought the Britons, killed three kings and took control of three cities. Another battle took place in 628 AD

The Thames Valley has been the site of numerous finds of ancient artefacts from a number of periods. Roman pottery has been found at many sites.

These Roman artefacts were found at Headington near Oxford in the nineteenth century.

and was between Penda of Mercia and Ceadwalla, King of North Wales, who fought Cynegils, King of Wessex. There was supposedly so much slaughter that despite neither side winning, they made peace. Also, in 879 AD, Guthrum's army stayed in the area for a year after being beaten by Alfred. They then moved to East Anglia.

TWO

From the Normans to the Nineteenth Century

The arrival of the Normans led to a major change in the method of defending the Thames. At first, the incidents of attacks by foreign powers sailing up the Thames declined and the arrival of the castle changed the face of some parts of the river. Although castles were built principally to control the surrounding countryside, they also existed to protect the river.

The incidents of foreign attacks occurred again when the French raided some of the towns along the river, including Gravesend in 1380. This led to building part of the Thames's early defences that still exist in some form today. The later Dutch

The Tower of London was originally built by William the Conqueror and was one of a number of castles close to the Thames.

The remains of a thirteenth-century gate tower at the Tower of London.

attack in 1667, when they got as far as the Medway, indicated that the country needed to undertake even more precautions to help defend the settlements on the Thames.

The majority of the action on the river during this period of history actually occurred further upriver. West of London was the prime site for battles during the Civil War, specific examples being Brentford, Reading and Oxford.

One of the strangest events to occur on the river in this post-Hastings period may have been one of the first experiments of using a submarine. William Bourne, a British mathematician, made plans for a submarine in 1578. In 1620, however, a Dutchman, Cornelius van Drebbel, actually built one. He wrapped a wooden rowing boat in leather and had air tubes held on the surface by floats. The submarine was powered by twelve oarsmen and stayed submerged for three hours.

ESTUARY

There seems to have been little naval action during the Civil War, perhaps due to the fact that the navy was mainly loyal to Parliament for much of the war. There was, however, a confrontation between Parliamentary and Royalist ships in the Thames in 1648 when King Charles I was already a prisoner.

There were a number of land-based rebellions against Parliament during 1648. This was after victory had seemed to have been won by the New Model Army. There was also some unrest among the crews of ships at Chatham after dissent at Rochester.

A revolt among the crews of ships off the coast of Kent led to a declaration that they wanted an agreement made with the king. Nine ships sailed to Holland to put themselves at the disposal of the Prince of Wales. The fleet then carrying Prince Charles sailed around the South Coast trying to incite an uprising. When this failed, the Prince lost heart and decided to return to Holland.

Parliament had acted by this time and a fleet of eleven ships, commanded by the Earl of Warwick, were ready to sail on the Thames. A number of the ships in Prince Charles's fleet ignored their leader's return to Holland and sailed up the Thames. The two fleets anchored close to each other on the river before the Royalist ships turned and followed the Prince back to Holland, duly followed at a distance by Warwick's fleet.

SHEERNESS

A blockhouse was built at Sheerness in the reign of Henry VIII, along with a number of others on the Thames. The blockhouse was later replaced by a fort, which was begun in 1667. It was supposedly armed with eighteen guns but was poorly provisioned and manned by local militia. The fort was destroyed by the Dutch when they attacked in 1667. When the Dutch landed further along the coast, the garrison fired one salvo. Many of the guns at the fort fell off their carriages when fired in retaliation – they had not been well maintained and the men of the fort then fled. Sheerness has the distinction of being the last fort in the country to fall to an enemy since artillery was invented.

When the Dutch arrived at Sheerness, Sir Edward Spragg was in command of the few British ships in the area. They did not put up much of a defence – the frigate *Unity* fired one broadside at the Dutch and then retreated.

A much larger fort designed by Bernard de Gomme, who also designed Tilbury Fort, was built at Sheerness after the Dutch attack. The new fort was built to protect against attacks from the sea, the Medway and on land. The fort also contained barracks and a chapel.

An old drawing of English ships and their captains.

QUEENSBOROUGH

The castle at Queensborough on the Isle of Sheppey, built by Edward II at a cost of £25,000, was originally intended to defend against invasion or attack by the French. It was also believed that some very early guns were installed at the castle.

The site became a favourite residence of Edward III and was named in honour of his wife, Queen Philippa. Edward III first visited the castle in 1361 and often returned there by boat from Hadleigh.

The castle was attacked in 1450 by Jack Cade's army. It held out against them with a garrison of just twenty-two men. Although upgraded during the reign of Elizabeth I, the castle was ultimately destroyed during the Civil War.

MEDWAY

Chatham had never grown much beyond a small settlement until Henry VIII built his dockyard there. He was responsible for an enormous expansion in the navy, increasing the number of ships from single figures to more than a hundred. This number of ships needed to be maintained and it was decided to do this at Chatham.

As the dockyard at Chatham became more important, the local population grew to service it. It also needed to be defended, and one of the first fortifications built to

Upnor Castle was built during the reign of Elizabeth I to help protect Chatham Dockyard. Its garrison put up some resistance against the attack from the Dutch in the seventeenth century.

protect it was Upnor Castle. It was designed to hold artillery as early as the sixteenth century by order of Elizabeth I.

When the Duke of Albemarle arrived at Chatham to fight the Dutch during the attack of 1667, he found that the large workforce at the dockyard had almost completely vanished. He ordered artillery to be brought up from Gravesend. Upnor was, however, one of the few defences to put up a fight against the Dutch when they sailed into the Medway. It was probably the resistance from Upnor that persuaded the Dutch to leave the area.

Cockham Wood Fort was built close to Upnor in 1668 as a result of the Dutch raid. During the eighteenth century, a number of further defences were built to protect Chatham from a potential land-based attack. These were the Cumberland Lines, a structure of ditches and ramparts that included a number of forts, such as Fort Amherst and Fort Townsend. The defences included a number of tunnels dug out of the cliffs and used for magazines.

LEIGH-ON-SEA

Hadleigh Castle, which is now a ruin, was built close to Leigh by Hubert de Berg when he was Regent to the young King Henry III in 1219. By 1228, the king had fallen out with de Berg, but Hadleigh Castle was still completed under his guidance. It was to be used as a defence for London against the French to stop them using the Thames as a means of carrying out raids.

After de Berg's death in 1243, the king took possession of the castle but it fell into ruin. Edward III began to renovate the castle and added towers and a barbican. When Edward was in residence, there were often jousting tournaments held on the green. In later years, the castle was given to three of his wives as a gift by Henry VIII.

The castle also overlooked the gathering of large English fleets – one fleet that went to fight the Armada sailed from close to the castle. Another fleet that went to fight the Dutch sailed from the then large naval port of Leigh. The castle itself never faced any enemies and, by the sixteenth century, it was sold, stone by stone. Much of what was left then fell into the river, owing to subsidence.

In Elizabethan times the area around Leigh Creek was well-known for shipbuilding. As warships got larger, the industry in the area declined. The connection with the navy continued, however, and during the seventeenth century a number of the inhabitants of Leigh became well-known high-ranking members of the navy.

Probably the best-known of these naval families were the Haddocks. Sir Richard Haddock was an admiral and fought the Dutch in the wars of the seventeenth century. Sir Richard was followed in the rank by his son Nicholas, in the early eighteenth century.

CANVEY ISLAND

When the Dutch attacked the Thames in 1667, Canvey was one of the places they landed. They burned the church there and stole cattle. Not everyone living in the area tried to resist the invaders. One local man did just the opposite.

John Gentbridge was accused of joining the Dutch and coming ashore to plunder the house of Joseph Cole of Canvey Island. Gentbridge then supposedly piloted the Dutch ships into the Thames, which allowed them to attack Sheerness and the Medway.

COOLING CASTLE

Cooling Castle owes its origins to the French raid on Gravesend in 1380. John de Cobham reinforced a house on the site to provide some level of defence. Previous castles had arrow slits, but Cooling installed gun ports, which were arrow slits with a round hole at the bottom. This gave them the look of upside-down keyholes. One of the men who worked on the castle was the stonemason Henry Yevele, who also worked on the Tower of London.

The castle may have been built to defend the Thames, but it was at more risk from land attacks. It was once seized by Richard II and later fell to Sir Thomas Wyatt during the revolt against Queen Mary in 1554. Cannon were used to break open the gates and the owners, the Cobham family, were forced to join the rebellion.

COALHOUSE FORT

The fort at Coalhouse Point was originally one of Henry VIII's blockhouses. This was built about half a mile from where the present fort stands. There was another blockhouse across the river at Higham, providing a crossfire with the fortification at East Tilbury. The Essex blockhouse was armed with fifteen cannon, then updated a few years later and remained until the defence fell into disuse. It was derelict by the time the Dutch attacked during 1667.

The nearby church supposedly sustained damage to its tower from Dutch fire. This is disputed by some, who claim that the fire actually came from English ships. Others claim that the church did not have a tower to begin with.

The area was re-fortified at the end of the eighteenth century when the Napoleonic Wars began. A twenty-four-gun battery was built, along with barracks for the garrison.

GRAVESEND

Gravesend was sacked by the French in 1380 and was fortified thereafter. Blockhouses were built during the reign of Henry VIII. These were part of a series of defences built by the king. This included castles along the South Coast and smaller blockhouses at other points, including on the Thames in 1539.

The cost of building the defences was quite high, so to save money it is believed that Henry used land taken from the Church to build his Thames defences. The sites in Gravesend had been medieval hospitals that had declined into chapels or chantries during the fourteenth and fifteenth centuries. It was on these sites that the blockhouses were built.

There were two blockhouses at Gravesend, whose construction employed fourteen masons at 8*d* a day, ten at 4*d* and twelve labourers at 6*d*. The blockhouses

Some of the early defences at Gravesend, that developed through the years.

at Gravesend were commanded by Captains Crane and Cobham. One of the defences was built at Milton and the other at Gravesend; the Gravesend blockhouse being close to the Clarendon Royal Hotel. Part of the hotel was originally the Duke of York's quarters. At the time of writing, the hotel was itself undergoing redevelopment.

When the Dutch attacked in 1667 it seems that the only defences that were fully operational this far up the Thames were the blockhouses at Gravesend and Tilbury. If the Dutch had been aware of how weak these were, they may have been more willing to sail further along the Thames than they did.

Samuel Pepys made an inspection tour of Gravesend and reported how unprepared it was for defending potential invasion. The Duke of Albemarle took command and new defences were built. This seems to have included Trinity Fort, but little is known about this or its whereabouts. The fort seems to have had a short lifespan and was neglected during a later reorganisation of the defences at Gravesend and Tilbury.

It was not until the late eighteenth century that further defences were added to Gravesend. Thomas Page made a survey of the Thames defences in 1778, recommending a new battery, which was to become the New Tavern Fort; it could hold fifteen guns.

The grounds of the Clarendon Hotel was the site of one of Henry VIII's blockhouses. Part of the building was the headquarters of the Duke of York. The photograph of the building is from the rear, when the hotel was undergoing renovations in 2007.

The defences of the Thames at Gravesend were not only subject to damage by enemy action. In December 1790, a violent storm struck the Thames and the *Albion* and the *Taunton Castle* were driven ashore. The *Carnatic* had her main topmast carried away and the mainmast was struck by lightning. Hot pitch from the rigging then ran between the decks and set fire to the ship.

TILBURY

Tilbury had been identified as a site that needed to be defended as early as 1539. A blockhouse was built there opposite those built at Gravesend. The commander was Captain Grant and he was paid 12*d* a day. The rest of the force consisted of a second in command at 8*d* per day, a porter at 6*d*, two soldiers at 6*d*, and four gunners at 6*d*. The blockhouse was not only armed with cannon but also with a stock of bows and arrows.

The site of the blockhouse, which later became the fort, had previously been a medieval hospital. In turn the hospital became a chantry, taken over by the king and used as the site for his new defences.

In 1588, a large army assembled at Tilbury under the command of the Earl of Leicester to meet any Spanish troops landed by the Armada. Leicester found the defences there in a very poor condition. The army at Tilbury was visited by Queen Elizabeth I, who made the famous speech when she is reputed to have said, 'I may have the weak and feeble body of a woman, but I have the heart and stomach of a king.'

To enable the forces at Tilbury to cross the river quickly if the Spanish landed in Kent, a bridge was built across the river mounted on boats. There was also a boom in front of the bridge built with chains and cables to stop ships coming upriver.

The gathering of such a large army was not without problems for the locals. The church close to the camp had its wall broken down and the stones used as stoves while stools from the church were used for firewood. The church even lost its men, as the churchwardens went off to join the army.

The Water Gate at Tilbury Fort is one of the most elaborate features of any of the Thames defences.

Infantry firing positions at Tilbury Fort. This runs parallel to the main gate, giving it covering fire.

One strange event connected with the army involved a man named Thomas Cockerell, who was about to be married in Colchester. The captain of the force he was attached to arrived at the church and took him back to Tilbury before the marriage took place.

From the early seventeenth century, the governor of the fort also took control of the ferry. It was later decided that the governor should be responsible for the repair of the road leading to the river crossing and this was to be paid for out of the profits from the ferry.

The danger to the garrison at the fort did not only come from the enemy. In July 1650, Richard Pitman, a soldier from the fort, was killed by a gun at an alehouse at the bottom of the hill in West Tilbury.

The fort at Tilbury was mentioned by Daniel Defoe in his tour of the eastern counties in 1722. He described the fort as 'the key to the Thames' and consequently 'the key to London'. He thought that the ornate Water Gate was noble, but that the fort was far from just cosmetic and that the crew of any ship willing to pass the guns there must be bold fellows. The commander of the fort at the time was Lord Newbrugh

Defoe's words were to be relevant for some time, as in 1766 the fort still held fifty-six guns. At that time it was the only fortified place on the Thames in Essex. To test the strength of the defences, 5,000 troops crossed the river in 1780 and set up camp behind the fort. They then carried out a mock attack on the walls.

During the Nore Mutiny of 1797, Tilbury was one of the places where troops were stationed in case the mutiny should escalate. The 49th Regiment of Foot and the Warwickshire Militia were based there.

PURFLEET

The banks of the Thames were the site of a number of gunpowder magazines. In the early years their construction was mainly unrestricted, but in 1772 an Act of Parliament made it illegal to make gunpowder without a licence. All magazines on the Thames also had to be below Blackwall after the act came into force.

The Purfleet magazine was positioned close to the Royal Hotel on the riverbank. It was built in 1760 and was intended to replace the magazine at Woolwich. There were five magazine buildings which could hold over 10,000 barrels of gunpowder. Much of the powder at Purfleet came from the mills at Waltham Abbey and was carried by barge along the River Lea and the Thames.

The magazine had a famous visitor soon after it was built. Benjamin Franklin was a member of the Royal Society and was asked to suggest what should be done about lightning safety at the magazine. There was a disagreement over whether the lightning conductors on the buildings should be rounded or pointed. The disagreement seemed to be based on political rather than scientific differences, as Franklin had been involved in the American War of Independence and was not popular with all his fellow members.

Lightning was a common worry at the magazine. During a terrible storm in December 1790 there were several lightning strikes along the Thames. This raised serious worries at Purfleet as the consequences of a strike could have been catastrophic.

BARKING

Barking was once the site of a famous abbey that was one of the largest landowners in the area. The abbey stood by the River Roding, a short distance from the Thames. The abbey buildings were often used to house a number of important people. William the Conqueror lived at the abbey while the Tower of London was under

Engraved for Harrison's History of London &c.

The bishops and citizens of England swearing fealty to William after the Battle of Hastings.

construction. There are rumours that while he was there, his army lived at a camp on ancient earthworks further along the River Roding at Uphall.

The Roding was an important route for transporting timber from Hainault Forest. This was in the days when warships were made from English oak and the logs were floated down the Roding to the Thames, then up to the royal dockyards at Deptford and Woolwich.

WOOLWICH

Woolwich dockyard was also founded in the reign of Henry VIII and was first used for the building of the ship *Henry Grace a Dieu* in 1514. As well as the dockyard, an ordnance depot was founded during Henry's reign, which was later to become the Royal Arsenal.

During the 1770s, the ordnance department built a large barrack building close to the arsenal and shipyard on Woolwich Common. The department were responsible for defensive structures and artillery. It was one of the largest residential buildings in the country in those days.

Barracks were quite rare at the time. Most fighting was carried out during the summer and large army camps were set up on a temporary basis when there was a danger of invasion. The French Wars of the late eighteenth century changed this, as the size of the army grew, somewhere had to be found to house them and barracks began to appear.

GREENWICH

It was the wife of William III, Queen Mary, who was responsible for the Royal Naval Hospital at Greenwich. The first brick was laid in 1695 and, for more than 150 years, veterans of the British Navy lived out their final days at the hospital. The building actually took place after Mary's death, perhaps partly as a tribute by her husband. It was long thought that England should pay its debt to its sailors for their service, but it was the queen's input that turned an idea into reality.

A drawing of a sixteenth-century English sailor. It was to be many years after this that sailors were finally given uniforms.

Greenwich Hospital was the idea of Queen Mary, wife of William III. It was finally built in 1695, after her death.

Built on the site of the royal palace, the hospital cared for seamen who were disabled by age or wounds received in service. It also cared for the widows and children of those who had died in the service of their country.

DEPTFORD

It was Henry VIII who reorganised the navy and another of the dockyards he founded was at Deptford. There was also a Corporation of Trinity House formed at Deptford in 1514, which was responsible for making and erecting beacons and signs to help ships avoid hazards and make their way into port. The dockyard was begun in 1517.

It is interesting to note the details of a captain of a large ship's pay of that time. The *Gabryell Royall* was a ship of 800 tons with a crew of 420. In 1513 the captain, Sir William Trevellian, was paid 18*d* per day.

Deptford was once the site of the old Naval Victualling Yard. It was at Deptford that Queen Elizabeth knighted Sir Francis Drake in 1580 on the deck of his ship, the *Golden Hind*, after he had sailed around the world. It was also one of the shipyards that built the 'wooden walls' of England that helped to defeat the Armada.

LONDON

After the Normans arrived there were few foreign threats to the capital. Although many of the coastal towns were regularly attacked by foreign ships, London was in a more secure position. That was until it was attacked by its own people. After the third poll tax was introduced in 1381, large groups of men from Kent and Essex approached London, supposedly led by Wat Tyler. The city was still surrounded by walls at the time, so someone must have let them enter, and it is now thought that a number of Londoners supported the men and even joined them. Once inside

An early drawing of London Bridge showing the tower to defend its entrance on the south side of the river.

During the rebellion led by Wat Tyler, one of the buildings destroyed was the Savoy Palace, owned by John of Gaunt.

the walls, the men released the incarcerated from several prisons. They destroyed a number of buildings including the Savoy Palace owned by John of Gaunt

After meeting the king at Greenwich, the result was a further engagement at Mile End where Wat Tyler was killed. Meanwhile, other rebels managed to get into the Tower of London and killed a number of officials, including Sir Robert Hales, John Legge, William Appleton, Richard Somenour and Archbishop Sudbury. All were beheaded on Tower Hill.

The banks of the Thames were adorned with a number of large houses and palaces. These were the homes of the gentry and royalty during the Middle Ages. The view from the roof of Arundel House gives some idea of what London looked like then. The fate of the Savoy Palace, however, shows how these large palaces could become targets in revolts by the lower orders.

Although King Richard II had agreed to the demands of the rebels once the danger was over, he duly cancelled his previous agreements; the rebels were hunted down in their hometowns and many were put to death.

During the Civil War, there were attempted attacks on London by the king. He marched towards the capital from Oxford in 1643. His progress was stopped by the bands of trained London men who were a type of militia; early in the war they were Parliament's most reliable force. In 1642/3 around 20,000 of London's population built an 18ft high and 9ft thick rampart around the city.

One of the best-known figures in seventeenth-century London, Samuel Pepys, began his naval career on 23 March 1660 when he went on board one of the ships waiting in the river below the Tower to go and retrieve Charles II from Holland.

Pepys was to stay in London to carry out his duties at the Navy Board in 1665, despite the Black Death raging in the streets around him. By this time, war had been

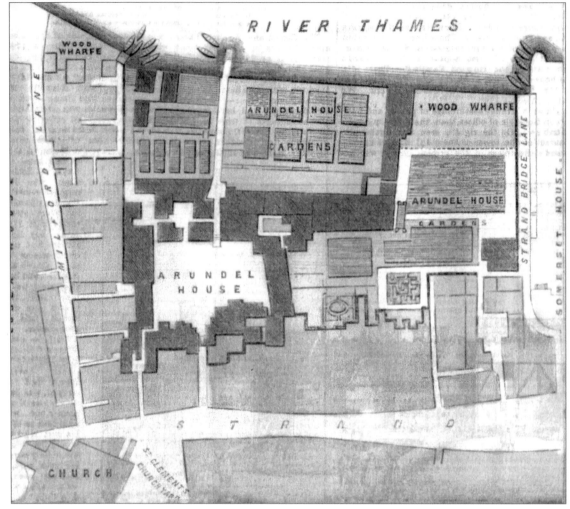

The plan of Arundel House shows the size of these palaces along the river. It is hard to imagine a private house covering this much space in central London nowadays.

declared against the Dutch and, despite some notable victories, there was no money to pay the wounded sailors who lay outside his office.

The problems of his office were again serious the following year, when the Great Fire of London threatened Pepys's home and office. He had to escape with his belongings by boat from Tower Pier.

PUTNEY

The town of Putney played some part in the Civil War: Cromwell had an encampment there for a time. The church in the town was the scene of a council of war in 1647 when Fairfax, Ireton, Rich and Fleetwood sat around the communion table with their hats on. The treatment of religious buildings was less than respectful during the war, and some were even used as prisons or stables. There was a bridge, fortified at each end, constructed from connecting boats, across the river at Putney during the Civil War.

CHISWICK

Chiswick was also used to plan movements during the Civil War – Cromwell having held a council at the Bull's Head Tavern at Strand on the Green. In November 1642, Charles I won a battle at Brentford and the Earl of Essex brought his Parliamentary Army of 24,000 men to Turnham Green. The Earl rode from regiment to regiment to encourage his men. They reportedly threw their caps in the air and cried 'Hey for old Robin'.

The Parliamentary Army attacked a group of Royalists at Acton. There was not an early battle, as Essex was waiting for the rest of his army to arrive. The Royalists did not wait – they retreated, leaving a small force of cavalry. The cavalry were then attacked by the Parliamentary artillery and rejoined the rest of their forces.

Tower Hill was famous as the site of public executions throughout the Middle Ages. This memorial marks the spot of the scaffold and the plaques list the names of those executed there.

BRENTFORD

After winning the Battle of Edgehill, the Royalist Army marched on London. They attacked the Parliamentary forces at Brentford and overcame them. A number of the members of the Parliamentary forces were driven into the Thames and were drowned. The Royalists also sunk two boats full of Parliamentary reinforcements. They planned to move on to take the Parliamentary artillery at Hammersmith. The Earl of Essex then moved his forces from London to Turnham Green and the Royalist army retreated.

KINGSTON UPON THAMES

There was an old manor house at Kingston that was often called the castle, so it may have been crenellated at some time. It was owned by the De L'isle family in the mid-eleventh century.

The town was fought over in the Wars of the Roses and the Civil War. Lord Francis Villiers was killed there during a skirmish in 1648. Even after Charles I was captured and held prisoner at Carisbrooke, Lord Holland and the Duke of Buckingham recruited around 600 men in support of the king and made Kingston their base. They were defeated on Surbiton Common and the Civil War finally ended.

HAMPTON COURT

Cardinal Wolsey was responsible for building much of Hampton Court and surrounded the palace with a moat. Defending houses had as good as died out by

Hampton Court Palace became too grand and was coveted by the king. Perhaps this was why the palace was built with a moat.

the Wars of the Roses, so the moat was quite unusual for the period. The Civil War was to lead to a return to the previous method of defending houses, so perhaps the moat was not such an unusual idea. Oliver Cromwell often stayed at Hampton Court and Charles I was kept prisoner there.

RUNNYMEDE

The rebelling barons met at Bury St Edmunds in November 1214 to plan their actions against King John, who had just been defeated at the Battle of Bouvines in France, because promises made to them by the king had been broken. The group included Robert Fitzwalter, whose daughter had allegedly been poisoned by King John. Robert de Ros, Gilbert de Clare, Robert de Percy, Geoffrey de Mandeville, Henry Bohun and William de Malet were also present.

Runnymede was a council meadow in Saxon times. Perhaps this was why it was chosen as the site to sign Magna Carta.

They approached John at London after he fled from Worcester. He asked for time to consider their claims, which they presented to him. They returned to him at Easter when he refused to give in to them. The population were obviously on the side of the barons, as every town they approached threw open the gates and joined them. John then acceded to their demands.

An old print commemorating the signing of Magna Carta. The image of the king is from his tomb at Worcester. The image of Fitzwalter is from his seal and the view is of Runnymede.

The meeting between King John and the barons went on for many days on Magna Carta Island and resulted in the king signing the Magna Carta – an event he was far from happy with.

It is believed that Runnymede meant 'council meadow' in Anglo-Saxon times. It is also believed that Edward the Confessor held his Witan there. Magna Carta Island was where King John was forced to sign the agreement drawn up by his subjects. The meetings before the document was signed took several days and the king stayed at Windsor, returning to the island every morning. John was supposedly very angry at being forced to sign and cursed the mother who bore him, wishing that he had died by the sword instead.

After signing the Magna Carta, John placed himself at the head of an army of foreign mercenaries and laid waste to large parts of the country. The barons then offered the crown to Louis, the son of the French king, and he landed with an army. After John's death, the Earl of Pembroke opposed the barons and the French prince, and Henry II became king.

WINDSOR

Windsor was one of William the Conqueror's castles, although there were supposedly fortifications on the site well before his arrival and a number of additions to the site were carried out by various later monarchs. Edward III was born at Windsor and it was always popular with him. Edward had great ideas of chivalry, despite the savage treatment he often meted out to captives in the wars during his reign. He was influenced by the idea of King Arthur and his Knights of the Round Table. There was even a belief that Windsor Castle had originally been built by Arthur.

Windsor was one of William's castles but found favour with Edward III, who was responsible for extending the building.

In the 1340s, Edward decided to rebuild the castle. He planned to include a round table and found an order of 300 knights. The castle was rebuilt, but the round table never was. The order was founded and turned out to be the Order of the Garter. The garter in question was supposedly dropped by the Countess of Salisbury during a dance. The king picked it up and put it round his own knee.

The castle was also used as an elite prison when a prisoner of war was held for ransom. King John of France was held at the castle at the same time as King David of Scotland, who was captured after the battle at Neville's Cross. It was supposedly those two who suggested further adaptations to the building to Edward III. He agreed and decided that their ransoms should pay for the building work.

The castle was occupied by Parliamentarians in 1642 and political prisoners were kept there. Under the orders of the Commandant, Colonel Veen, the chapel was despoiled and the deer in the park were killed. Cromwell was there in 1645 and Charles I was held as a prisoner. The secret funeral of Charles I was held at Windsor – his headless body was brought there by Bishop Juxon and buried.

HENLEY

Henley was the site of many conflicts during the Civil War and there were a number of fortified manor houses in the area that became involved. Greenland House was the base of a Royalist force and was besieged for almost six months by Parliamentary troops until captured in July 1644. Fawley Court was almost completely destroyed by Cromwell's men and Phyllis Court was held by 300 supporters of Parliament.

The bridge across the river at Henley was also destroyed during the Civil War and had to be replaced with a drawbridge.

READING

The town of Reading was the site of an early Norman Castle. It was supposedly built by King Stephen but the site has now completely disappeared. Reading Abbey was the burial place of royal personages including Henry I and William, son of Henry II. Many of the royal tombs were destroyed when the abbey was dissolved in 1539. Hilaire Belloc said of the abbey, 'the massiveness of its structure and type of architecture resembled that of Durham.'

The town was also the site of a number of parliaments, at various times, during the reign of Elizabeth I, for example, when the court fled an outbreak of plague in London.

After winning the Battle of Edgehill in 1642, the Royalist Army approached London but were held at Turnham Green – they then retreated to Reading. There were some attempts at a peace treaty, but these failed. The town was then besieged by Lord Essex for the Parliamentary forces in April 1643.

Essex's army marched from Windsor on 13 April. Reading was an important base for the Royalists as it commanded the Thames and the garrison of around 2,000 was commanded by Sir Arthur Aston. Stone from the abbey was used to reinforce the town walls, which added to the building's decline.

The Parliamentary Army numbered 16,000 men and arrived at Reading on 14 April. Essex took Caversham Bridge to stop reinforcements reaching the town, though some reinforcements did arrive by river. Aston was wounded and his second in command, Richard Fielding, arranged a truce and agreed to surrender on 25 April.

An old print of William the Conqueror, whose arrival changed the face of the country, including the banks of the Thames.

A Royalist force led by the King and Prince Rupert arrived at this time and attacked the Parliamentary forces holding Caversham Bridge. Fielding refused to help them as he had already called a truce. The reinforcements returned to Oxford, followed by the garrison from Reading, who had been allowed to leave. On arrival at Oxford, Fielding was court-martialled and sentenced to death. The sentence was never carried out. The Parliamentary troops marched into the town after the Royalists left and spent two days plundering Reading before order was restored.

Reading was once again involved in rebellion and was the site of a battle won by William of Orange in 1688. The town had been garrisoned by the Irish troops of James II. The Irish were very unpopular in the town and there were rumours that the soldiers were going to massacre the population. This tipped the balance of the town in favour of the Protestants – when the Count of Nassau sent 300 men to the town, they were supported by the townsmen in defeating the royal troops.

WALLINGFORD

The fortified town of Wallingford and its bridge was put to use by William the Conqueror. It was where he crossed the Thames and camped before moving round to approach London from the North. Robert d'Oyley later built a castle on a mound near the river. The castle was later used by Matilda, who was besieged here by King Stephen during the war between them.

The town was often the site of royal meetings and, in particular, Henry II held a council at Wallingford after his accession to the throne. King John also held a conference here with his barons and gave the castle to his son Richard in 1308. Joan, the wife of the Black Prince, died in Wallingford Castle.

The town was also used during the Civil War, as Colonel Blagge removed the centre of the bridge and replaced it with a drawbridge to improve its defences in

Earthworks at Wallingford which are thought to date from the Civil War.

1641. The castle was an important Royalist stronghold. It was one of the last places to hold out for the king, which was probably why Cromwell decided to destroy the building. A few remnants can still be seen down by the river.

ABINGDON

Men from Abingdon served with King Harold at Hastings when he fought William the Conqueror. Godric was the Sheriff of Fyfield and held his land from Abingdon Abbey. His wife was the keeper of Edward the Confessor's hounds at Abingdon. Godric died during the Battle of Hastings. Another local man, Thurkill, also held lands from the abbey and also died with Harold.

There were several skirmishes in the area during the Civil War. Abingdon was taken by Lord Essex and left under the command of Waller. It was during this period that the Abingdon Cross was destroyed.

OXFORD

The name Oxford came from the ford across the Thames that farmers used for their oxen. After the Battle of Hastings, Robert d'Oyley was given Oxford by William the Conqueror. He had a causeway built across the Thames and built a wall around the town, replacing earthen ramparts. In keeping with Norman style in other towns, d'Oyley flattened houses in the town to make space for his castle with a moat.

The castle was built in 1071 to control the town and the property of d'Oyley. This original building would have been of wood and earth, in keeping with most of the early Norman castles. It is thought that the stone tower of St George was also built by d'Oyley.

The castle and town was attacked during the war between Stephen and Matilda in 1142. Stephen took the town and then besieged Matilda in the castle for three months. Matilda supposedly escaped in the snow, camouflaged in white clothes at Christmas, along with three of her men. She crossed the Thames, which was frozen, and got away to Abingdon.

There was another attack during the Barons' Revolt in 1215; the attack was by King John and the castle was held by the rebel barons. It was finally taken in 1216 and repaired and improved by adding a barbican.

In keeping with other castles, it became less important as a defensive structure and was used as a prison during the sixteenth century. In the following century the castle once again became a stronghold during the occupation of the town by the forces of Charles I during the Civil War. After the Battle of Edgehill in 1642, which the king won, the Royalists headed for London. If they had reached the capital first, they may have won the war but the defeated army of Lord Essex got there first.

The Royalist Army got as far as taking Brentford and Charles had planned to live at Windsor, but later they were held up at Turnham Green by the Parliamentary Army. The Royalists retreated and Oxford became the base for Royalist forces for four years. The town was also protected by Royalist defences at Wallingford, Abingdon and Faringdon.

The castle at Oxford was built by Robert d'Oyley, one of William's men. It played a part in the war between Stephen and Matilda.

After playing a part in a number of conflicts, the castle at Oxford became part of the prison.

After the fall of Reading in April 1643 the Parliamentary Army, led by the Earl of Essex, looked set to march on Oxford. There was also another Parliamentary Army led by Sir William Waller, on its way to support Essex. Waller was delayed by a Royalist victory in Cornwall and Essex's army was struck by illness while encamped at Thame.

Prince Rupert led several raids on Essex's army. One of theses sorties was aimed at stealing a convoy and bringing the money to pay the Parliamentary forces, but they were unable to find it. A Parliamentary force followed Prince Rupert, who then ambushed and defeated them at Chalgrove. Oxford was to hold out for some time after this and finally surrendered in June 1646.

During the Royalist spell in the town, they melted down the gold and silver belonging to the colleges to pay for their war. The king's forces also used the lead roof of the cornmarket to make bullets, while Magdalen Grove became an artillery park and New College Cloisters became a gunpowder magazine. The students in the town were forced to spend one day a week building defences for the Royalist forces.

BAMPTON

Bampton Castle was supposedly built by King John but was more likely to have been constructed to the west of the town by Almer de Valance in the early fourteenth century. It may well have been built on the site of an earlier house. It remained in use as a manor house until the seventeenth century, when it partly fell into ruin. Some remnants did remain as part of a farmhouse called Ham Court.

RADCOT

The bridge at Radcot was one of the earliest on the Thames and may have been rebuilt after the battle of 1387 when Robert de Vere, the Earl of Oxford, was being pursued, along with his forces, by Henry Bolingbroke. When reaching Radcot, the bridge was broken and he had to swim with his horse across the river.

Earthworks known as the garrison, north of the bridge, are thought to be from the Civil War period when the Royalists held the town.

FARINGDON

Faringdon was the site of skirmishes in the wars of the eleventh century. Robert, Earl of Gloucester, built a castle during the reign of Stephen but it was later destroyed.

The town was a royal garrison in the Civil War and was one of the last places where the king's standard flew. The Royalists beat off a Parliamentary attack at Faringdon, but during this battle, the top of the church tower was lost to cannon fire.

CRICKLADE

Cricklade was the site of a Norman castle in the time of King Stephen. It was situated near Castle Hill, the site of an old Roman camp. There was also supposed to have been a hospital called St John's in the town, which cared for the wounded returning from the Crusades. The name of the first lock on the river derives from St John's Hospital.

CIRENCESTER

Cirencester played a part in several early conflicts. The town was attacked during the rebellion in King Stephen's time. It was also attacked and captured from the rebelling barons by Henry III.

Cirencester was a Parliamentary stronghold in the Civil War and was taken in 1642 by a Royalist Army under Prince Rupert. There were more than 300 deaths during the battle and more than a 1,000 of the population were held prisoner in the church and then marched to Oxford.

THREE

From Napoleon to the Twentieth Century

The strength of the defences on the Thames fluctuated during the nineteenth century. Although there was some building of a few new batteries during the Napoleonic Wars, the might of the navy was seen as a sufficient deterrent to attacks on the Thames.

The main growth of defensive building was in the middle of the century with the introduction of the Palmerston Forts. Unfortunately, once the danger that inspired the expansion passed, the defences were left to decline in a pattern that has been repeated throughout history.

In 1887, a letter to *The Times* noted the level of manpower at the five main forts in the Thames district responsible for defence of the capital. Coalhouse Fort had twenty heavy guns and was manned by a captain, master gunner and nine men. Tilbury had thirteen heavy guns and eight 10in howitzers manned by a lieutenant and twenty men. New Tavern Fort had fourteen heavy guns and one officer and fifteen men. Cliffe Fort had fourteen guns; Shornemead had thirteen guns and both were similarly undermanned.

It was not only forts on the banks of the river that changed during the nineteenth century. In 1842, Queen Victoria travelled by train from Windsor to London. The railway was to have a great effect on the river, as it offered a land-based alternative form of rapid transport. Speed of craft on the river had improved at the end of the eighteenth century with the invention of the paddle steamer. The nineteenth century was to see the battle between the paddle and the screw steamship – a battle which the screw propeller quickly won.

An article in the *Illustrated London News* in July 1854 stated that it was not long since those in high office said that it was not possible to propel warships through the water faster than 10 knots per hour. This was, of course, surpassed by screw steamers that carried troops and horses to the East. One screwship, the *Himalaya*, passed the 10-knot speed carrying a regiment of cavalry, large quantities of stores and baggage.

The *Warspite* training ship was moored off Woolwich from 1876 and had accommodation for 500 boys. The ship was destroyed by fire in 1918.

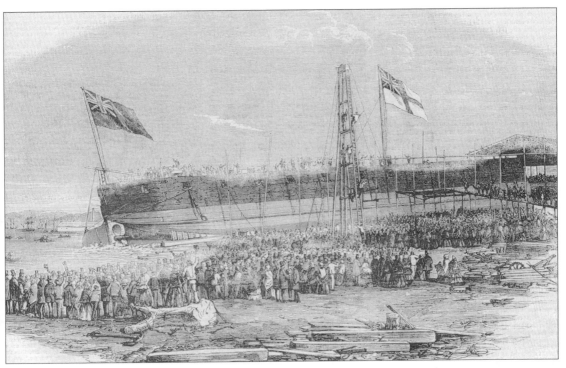

A number of new warships were launched on the Thames during the nineteenth century. The *Thunderbolt* was an iron steam battery made at Samuda's works at Millwall.

THE NORE

One of the best-known events of the early French Wars of this period were the mutinies that occurred among the navy in 1797. The first occurred off Spithead and was successful in gaining some improvements in naval conditions. A second mutiny took place among the fleet at the Nore, which was to be less successful, thus plunging the area along the Thames as far as London into a panic.

There were at least twenty ships involved in the mutiny at the Nore in 1797. Unlike the previous mutiny at Spithead, the Nore Mutiny took on a more political slant and the leader, Richard Parker, tried to use the ships involved to blockade London. Troops gathered at Gravesend, Sheerness and Tilbury. At one point, the guns at Shornemead battery fired on a group of mutineers in a cutter.

Richard Parker was a former schoolmaster who was serving time in a debtors' prison in Scotland when he was removed and sent to HMS *Sandwich* at Sheerness. Parker had previous naval experience and had been a midshipman. He had left the navy owing to illness after being demoted.

HMS *Sandwich* was a depot ship and was badly overcrowded. It was aboard this ship that the mutiny began. It quickly spread to other ships but initially was not taken too seriously by the Admiralty, as they expected it to end once the mutiny at Spithead was over. They were to be proved wrong.

Strangely, a number of the ships' officers involved stayed aboard their craft throughout the period of the mutiny. Officers who were not popular with the men, however, were sent ashore. One of these officers was a certain Captain William Bligh of HMS *Director*, formerly the captain of the *Bounty*.

The mutineers tried to get other ships at Gravesend and Long Reach on the Thames to join them. They also sent men to the North Sea Fleet at Yarmouth and a number of these ships did join the mutineers at the Nore. All the ships involved then gathered together at the Nore.

The eight demands of the mutineers were printed in *The Times* newspaper on 2 June. They were:

1.   That all the indulgences granted at Portsmouth be granted to all ships.
2.   That everyone should have leave when a ship comes into harbour.
3.   That all wages are paid before a ship goes back to sea.
4.   That any officer the mutineers had turned out of a ship would not be returned without the crew's permission.
5.   That new men would receive two months pay in advance to buy necessary items.
6.   That any men who deserted but are now again in naval service should not be taken as deserters.
7.   A more equal share of prize money
8.   To alter the 'Articles of War'.

By this time, the demands of the mutineers had been refused by the Admiralty and supplies to their ships were cut off. Troops were sent to Sheerness but the defences there were in a poor condition and the fort was hopeless as a defence for the arsenal. There were fears that the mutineers could sail up the river to attack London and, once past Sheerness, there was nothing much apart from Tilbury Fort to stop them. This magnified the lack of defences on the Thames.

The mutineers would often go ashore in the early days of the mutiny. They spent a lot of time at Sheerness but also went ashore at other places along the river. More troops were then sent to line the likely landing spots to stop the men leaving their ships, but this did not stop men going ashore to the Isle of Grain and the Isle of Sheppey to steal sheep for food.

The mutineers decided to enforce their attempts at gaining their goals by blockading the Thames. This sent shockwaves through the middle classes who used the river to trade. Volunteers came forward to fight the mutineers if they were needed and merchant ships were offered for this purpose. This included the fleet of the East India Company.

The failure to persuade the Admiralty to meet their demands led to the mutineers petitioning the king. They also gave a time limit on his answer and threatened to sail the ships to a foreign port if they were refused. To stop this happening, the buoys and beacons were all removed between them and the sea, though this left the alternative of sailing upriver towards London.

When their terms were again refused, an order was given to set sail but none of the ships did so. There were outbreaks of violence against some of the men and the officers still on the ships. After this, a number of the ships began to desert the cause. One got away while another went aground and was fired upon by the other ships.

As more and more craft began to be taken back into the command of their officers, many of the leaders tried to escape, knowing what was in store for them. A £500 reward was offered for the capture of Richard Parker. He was finally arrested aboard the *Sandwich* by men from the West Yorkshire Militia. One group of mutineers managed to get to Faversham, where they stole a ship and fled to France.

Parker was taken to Sheerness where he was booed by the locals. He was locked in the Black Hole under the chapel at the garrison. He was then sent to Maidstone Gaol. Parker was finally tried aboard the *Neptune* at Long Reach and sentenced to death. He was hanged aboard the *Sandwich*.

There were 400 other mutineers tried and of these, fifty-nine were sentenced to death, though only twenty-nine were executed. A further 180 were imprisoned on the *Eagle* hulk at Chatham.

In early August, the execution of four of the mutineers from the *Monmouth* was carried out on

An early map showing the Thames from Gravesend to the Nore.

board the ship. The four men, Vance, Frith, Brown and Earles, were hanged in front of the assembled crew. The men reportedly asked forgiveness for their actions and acknowledged the justice of their sentence. Brown allegedly informed the crew that they should take warning from his fate.

WHITSTABLE

During the Napoleonic Wars, a number of the French officers taken prisoner were allowed to live in towns around the country, away from the coast, on parole. They usually found their own lodgings and some worked, while others received money from home to supplement the amount they were paid by the British government. They were only allowed to travel a certain distance from the town and were authorised only to be out during certain hours, which varied according to the season.

Although they were released from captivity on their word of honour, not all of them lived up to this; a number of them escaped back to France. As a sideline to the smuggling of goods, some smugglers helped the escapees to get back to France at a price. One group that organised an escape route were based in Whitstable in Kent.

Boats from Whitstable regularly sailed across to the continent, even while the war was being fought. There was a system of travel to get the prisoners from whichever part of the country they were based in to Whitstable. Once there, they were hidden until they could be taken across to France.

SHOEBURYNESS

The artillery based at Shoeburyness included some very large guns. Shells from these larger guns could just reach Sheerness if pointed in the right direction. Any ships trying to enter the Thames would, therefore, have been well within their range.

The flag ship HMS *Duncan* at Sheerness. The *Duncan* was launched in 1811 and broken up in 1863.

The site was an important training base for members of the artillery. During October 1870, a division of the advanced class of gentlemen cadets studying at the Royal Military Academy at Woolwich were based at Shoeburyness. They were taking part in an instruction course at the school of gunnery under Colonel S.E. Gordon, the chief instructor. The class was under the command of Colonel G.A. Millman of the Royal Artillery.

SHEERNESS

Sheerness was surrounded with elaborate fortifications to protect the town and dockyard, which had been built over many years. The dockyard was used to get the smaller men-of-war ready for sea. There were also naval barracks in the town. The Isle of Sheppey was, however, one of the unhealthy areas of the Thames, and one of the last areas in Britain where the threat of malaria still existed.

This was perhaps unfortunate for the prisoners of war from the Crimea, who were confined aboard hulks at Sheerness in 1854. There were over 1,100 Russian and Finnish prisoners on board the *Devonshire* and the *Benbow*. They were taken at the fall of Bomarsund Fort in the Baltic Sea. After a spell on the hulks, they were later sent to prisons at Lewes and at Millbay in Plymouth.

The unhealthy atmosphere did little to affect how busy the dockyard was, judging by a report of arrivals at the yard in August 1856. The *Russell* came out of the fitting basin at Sheerness on 22 August and was immediately replaced by the six-screw steamship *Phoenix*. The ship was to be fitted for service.

The end of the Crimean War had an effect on manpower in the forces. The *Argus* paddle-wheel steamer was to be paid off at Sheerness on 26 August, as was the *Royal George* screw steamship on the 29th. At the same time there was an Admiralty order sent to the dockyard that all serving invalid pensioners were to be retired from active service. All long-serving pensioners were to undergo a medical to see if they were fit to continue in service, but would lose the extra 3*d* a day paid during the war.

While all this was going on, there was an accident at the dockyard. A boat from the *Trafalgar* capsized under the stern of the ship. A serving pensioner, John Griffiths, and a woman named Maycock were drowned. The man's body was found and was taken aboard the *Formidable* until the inquest. The woman's body was not recovered.

As well as repairing ships, Sheerness was also active in naval manoeuvres. A large naval battle took place in August 1887 between Admiral Freemantle's Division and D Division under Captain Long. Freemantle's force was to attack Sheerness but was opposed by the *Glatton* and the *Prince Albert*. Freemantle's force managed to evade them and headed for Sheerness.

Manoeuvres were not without risk and a gun on the *Curlew*, one of Freemantle's ships, caused an explosion of some blank shells. Four men were injured, Richard Blight, James Thompson, Alfred Brown and Frederick Stuart. The *Curlew* entered Sheerness to land the injured men but then was unable to take part in the rest of the manoeuvres.

The fort at Garrison Point was one of the Palmerston Forts of the mid-nineteenth century. It had replaced earlier forts, which included the one destroyed by the Dutch

Men-of-war at Sheerness. Sheerness was an important naval supply base and often took part in manoeuvres.

in the seventeenth century. The fort was planned to be protected by iron shields and have turrets on top, but these were never added.

During the nineteenth century there were numerous volunteer forces set up who would spend weekends and holiday periods training at camps. The Thames forts were well used by these volunteers, especially the artillery. In March 1888 the 2nd Kent Artillery Volunteers were stationed at Garrison Point Fort. They took over the duties of the Royal Artillery, who were based in the barracks at the fort.

The Kent Artillery volunteers had been the first to go into barracks for a few days each year. By 1888 they had been doing this for fifteen years. At Garrison Point they were based in the upper and lower casemates holding 25- and 18-ton guns.

The volunteers were led by Colonel Hughes MP. They had travelled by train from Woolwich to Port Victoria and from there the steamer *Cupid* had taken them to Sheerness Pier. They were led through the town by the band watched by large numbers of the local population.

The volunteers were able to practice on the 64-pounder muzzle-loading guns and the 40-pounder breechloaders mounted in the batteries facing the sea. They fired at targets nearly 2,000yds away from the shore. Not all the volunteers' time was spent working and leave was granted to visit the town.

Although hulks were used to hold prisoners of war during the Napoleonic Wars, the *Devonshire* was later brought into service at Sheerness to hold Russians captured during the Crimean War.

MEDWAY

Although the Medway is a tributary of the Thames, it obviously had a great effect on the defence of the river and was a target for attack. There were a number of defences built at different times. During the Napoleonic Wars, the defences added were mainly land-based to defend the shipyard at Chatham. These included the defences of Fort Pitt and Fort Clarence. Many of the river-based defences were from a much earlier period.

The new defences were known as the Cumberland Lines and were far from popular with the locals. This was mainly due to the ban on grazing animals on the lines. There was even a threat to kill Captain Brisac who was in command of the new defences.

Chatham was a major centre in the building of army barracks which were being expanded during the Napoleonic Wars. There were also several military hospitals in the area, some of which were visited by Queen Victoria and Prince Albert later in the century when they held wounded from the Crimea.

The nineteenth century was the heyday of large military displays and, at Chatham in July 1854, Prince Albert, along with numerous members of the public, watched the 35th Regiment use scaling ladders to attack the right face of Prince Henry's Bastion and establish themselves within the lines. The attackers were then themselves attacked by Royal Marines from Fort Amherst and driven out of the fortifications. Their retreat was then fired upon by the large guns of the King's Bastion.

The defensive structures on the Medway were often used as hospitals during the mid-nineteenth century. In July 1855, Queen Victoria visited many of the wounded men in various hospitals. Accompanied by Prince Albert, the queen visited Fort Pitt, which held 200 wounded. Those wounded but able to leave their beds, formed into

By the nineteenth century, many naval craft were steam-powered rather than sailing ships. Chatham was one of the shipyards still building them, as the launch of the *Cressy* screw ship in July 1853 shows.

Hoo Fort was one of a pair of Palmerston Forts (Darnet was the other) on opposite sides of the river. It was built in the mid-nineteenth century as protection for Chatham if the enemy should get past Sheerness.

Darnet was the second of a pair of forts (opposite Hoo fort) built in the mid-nineteenth century to protect Chatham.

two lines on the lawn. Each man held a card with details of his wound. The queen also went to the military hospital at Brompton Barracks, which held around 240 wounded. Many of these had just returned from the Crimea with frostbite.

In 1859 a Royal Commission recommended that a series of new forts and

Queen Victoria and Prince Albert visited Brompton Hospital in July 1854 where many of the patients had returned from the Crimea with frostbite.

Those able to leave their beds were paraded on the lawn at the hospital holding a card with the nature of their wound written on it.

batteries be built because of the political situation in Europe. There were also a number of volunteer forces recruited at the time, which included such famous units as the Artist Rifles. The new defences became known as Palmerston Forts and two of them were built on the islands of Hoo and Darnet, where there had been earlier batteries, to protect Chatham.

There were problems that were common in many Thames forts and the buildings began to crack because of the soft ground. As a result, the completed forts were often smaller than had originally been planned, but were more expensive than earlier estimates.

GRAIN FORT

Grain Tower was built in the mid-1850s and is only accessible by foot at low tide. Otherwise it can only be reached by boat. It is similar in design to the older Martello Towers. One difference to the Martellos was that Grain Tower was built to hold three guns, which was more than the original Martellos.

Although there were a number of batteries on Grain dating back to the seventeenth century, the fort was another of the Palmerston Forts of the mid-nineteenth century. The original plans had to be modified owing to subsidence at the site.

Grain Fort, in common with other Thames Forts, was often used for training by volunteer regiments. In March 1888 the 2nd Middlesex Artillery Volunteer Brigade were at Grain. A small party under the command of Captain Prager were the first to arrive. The main force was carried by train from London Bridge to the Grain crossing.

Grain Fort was another of the Palmerston Forts and was built to support Grain Tower. As well as the guns there were to be barracks for 250 men. The inset is of Shornemead.

Grain Tower was similar in design to the earlier Martello Towers when built, despite having been constructed much later. It was reached by a causeway at low tide or boat during high tide.

The fort was even more remote then than the area is now; in the dark the volunteers found it difficult to find the route along the muddy country roads. Because of the organisation of the commanding officer Colonel Keene, there was a meal and warm fires waiting for them when they arrived at 10 p.m.

The men were allowed to practice on the 9 in 12 ton, 10 in 18 ton and 11 in 25 ton guns. They also used the 64-pounder guns at one of the batteries. Targets were set in the river.

Not everyone took the volunteer camps seriously, and a report in some areas of the media had obviously described the volunteer camps as a holiday. There were accusations of cases of drunkenness. A letter from Lieutenant-Colonel Hope, the commander of the Brigade of Voluntary Artillery, to *The Times* in April 1877 was critical of this view. He argued that his men's time at Grain Fort was far from a holiday and he described their occupation of the defences as spent carrying out hard work and severe muscular exertion from a sense of duty and patriotism without any remuneration or compensation. The only reward that they could look for was that their efforts should be appreciated.

SLOUGH FORT

Slough was one of the first Palmerston Forts to be completed and was also one of the smallest. The fort was built in a D-shape and was to have a garrison of less than a hundred men.

In January 1872 it was reported that Slough was ready to have its armaments mounted. A detachment of men from the Royal Artillery at Sheerness were engaged to mount the weapons, which were described as very heavy guns.

CLIFFE FORT

Cliffe Fort was another Palmerston Fort which was to support Slough Fort, though it was much larger and had more guns and a garrison of around 300 men. The soft ground was a serious problem during construction of the fort. The marshy area was also very unhealthy, with the presence of malaria-carrying mosquitoes posing a serious risk.

The fort was used to mount a new wire-guided missile known as the Brennan Torpedo. The Fortification Bill of 1867–8 listed the expenditure on the Thames forts as £93,000, to be spent on Gravesend, Coalhouse, Cliffe, Shornemead and Slough Forts. There was £75,000 to be spent on the Medway and Sheerness Forts.

The construction of Cliffe Fort was to be dogged by subsidence owing to the marshy nature of the site. It was also very unhealthy as the district was still infested by malaria-carrying mosquitos.

COALHOUSE POINT

Coalhouse Fort was built in 1847, but there was a disagreement between the building contractor and Colonel Slade of the Royal Engineers. Slade thought that the contractor had a troublesome character. It took until 1855 to complete the fort

Coalhouse Fort was rebuilt in the middle of the nineteenth century and found to be out of date as soon as it was finished. It was rebuilt again a few years later.

but it was only to last six years. The developments in new weaponry made the new fort out of date almost as soon as it was complete.

What replaced it was one of the Palmerston Forts, built after recommendations by the Royal Commission in response to the situation in Europe in the mid-nineteenth century. It was one of a triangle of forts, the other two being on the Kent coast at Shornemead and Cliffe.

SHORNEMEAD FORT

Shornemead Fort was built in the mid-nineteenth century on the site of a Napoleonic battery. The fort was deemed to be unsuitable for its needs just as Coalhouse Fort had been, and a new fort was built a few years afterwards. As with other forts in the area, the soft ground caused problems with the structure that had been planned.

The main armament was facing the river. The rear of the fort consisted of barracks for the men. The fort also had a surrounding ditch with a drawbridge.

Shornemead Fort had a similar history to Coalhouse Fort. Constructed on the site of a Napoleonic battery in the late 1840s, it was found to be unsuitable in the 1860s and was rebuilt.

GRAVESEND

During the French Revolution, several people in Britain had sympathy for the French ideals. This led to some localities making declarations of support for the king, which is what happened with the Corporation at Gravesend, especially after the war began. In 1797, when the Nore Mutiny took place, the local volunteers were called out in the town in case of any conflict developing.

There were two forts in the area and Gravesend Fort, which dated from the time of Henry VIII, was updated in 1780 and again in 1795. By 1805 it had nineteen

Gravesend was one of the major ports for the embarkation of soldiers overseas. A report in the *Illustrated London News* in November 1846 explained the process for troops going abroad. The 3rd Regiment marched from Brompton Barracks and are led through Gravesend by the band.

Although there was a parting between some soldiers and their wives, twenty-two women and forty-three children were to accompany the men abroad.

The division consisted of 478 men under the command of Major Franklyn and Captain Hamilton. Of these, 275 men and the women and children were to go onboard the *Sybella* under Franklyn, while the rest went on the *Romeo* under Hamilton.

32-pounder guns. New Tavern Fort was built in 1779 during the American War of Independence. It was also updated in 1795 and, by 1805, it had two 32-pounders, fourteen 24-pounders and one 9-pounder.

Fort House was close to New Tavern Fort and was the home of General Gordon, of Khartoum fame, when he lived Gravesend. When he left, he donated the house and its grounds to the town. Part of the gardens are still known as Fort Gardens.

The men were rowed out to the ships and, when loaded, set sail for Ceylon.

Gravesend was one of the busiest ports for the embarkation of troops posted abroad in the mid-nineteenth century. In November 1846 the 3rd Regiment left for Ceylon. There were 478 men under the command of Major Franklyn and Captain Hamilton. The men had marched from Brompton Barracks to the town and 275 of the men along with ten women and twenty-five children were to sail on the *Sybella* under command of Captain Hamilton.

An account of an embarkation from Gravesend to India was also printed in the *Illustrated London News* of 21 November 1846. The men were led by a band from Chatham and passed beneath Fort Pitt. On reaching Gravesend, the men were loaded into a lumber boat and went alongside the *Gloriana*. Food for the men had already been prepared on board.

Each man's kit was held in a waterproof bag, secured with a strap and padlock. This was entirely useless as a security measure as all the padlocks were opened by the same key. This was a common occurrence. The East India Company soldiers were given chests known as Warley Boxes, which were also all opened by the same key.

There seems to have been a merry-go-round of postings at the numerous forts on the Thames. In December 1855, second-class staff surgeon George McCulloch of the 5th Dragoon Guards was ordered to New Tavern Fort to relieve staff surgeon J.K. Carr MD, who had been in charge of the troops' health at the fort. However, McCulloch could not have lasted long, as in August the following year staff surgeon E. Menzies was transferred from the hospital at Brompton Barracks to New Tavern Fort, not to relieve McCulloch, but an H. Mackay.

In January 1858, the Princess Royal and her consort, Prince Frederick William of Prussia, travelled to Gravesend to leave the country from Terrace Pier. The event was marked by a parade of several local regiments. One of the officers, Colonel Kelly, was described as the commandant of both Tilbury and New Tavern Forts.

In August 1862, the 1st Brigade of the Kent Volunteer Artillery, commanded by Lieutenant-Colonel Gladdish, were exercising on the 68-pounders and the 10 in guns at New Tavern Fort.

Embarkation from the port was continuous and in August 1870, Captain H. Dawson of the 75th Regiment embarked from Gravesend on the *Earl of Balcarres* to join the headquarters of his regiment in Bengal. Another officer obviously preferred not to travel on the ship from Gravesend. Captain H. Francis of the 64th Regiment received permission to travel to India overland instead of leaving from Gravesend.

In October 1870, the 30th Company Royal Engineers, commanded by Captain J.M. Maitland, left Woolwich by train bound for Gravesend. They were to complete a musketry course at the government rifle ranges at Milton. The families of the soldiers did not travel with them but stayed at Woolwich.

One of the large guns at New Tavern Fort.

A plaque commemorating General Gordon on the site of Fort House, which had been his home while based in Gravesend. The grounds of the house are now known as Fort Gardens and are part of the New Tavern Fort area.

TILBURY

Barracks were added to Tilbury Fort to help combat the fear of invasion in the early nineteenth century. To enable troops to cross from one side of the river to the other if needed, a tunnel was planned. Work was begun in 1803 but the task was obviously beyond the capabilities of the engineers and the tunnel was never completed.

The garrison at the fort was one of those claimed to be very weak; in 1849 the force was of sixty men who were invalided veterans. It was expected, however, that the fort could be fully manned within hours using steamers and men from the garrison at Woolwich.

During the Crimean War period, the main defence of the Thames moved closer to the sea, leaving Tilbury as part of the second line of defence. It was probably due to its less important role that Tilbury remained in such original condition. In 1868, General (Chinese) Gordon took control of the Thames forts with the task of updating them.

NORTHFLEET

September 1854 saw the launch of the gunboat *Pelter* at Northfleet. It was the first of four gunboats that had been ordered for the navy from Mr Pitcher of the Northfleet dockyard. The launch was attended by numerous officers from army and navy, as well as a number of ladies.

The ship was to armed with two guns of 95 cwt, which could fire solid balls of 8in diameter. Because of the shallowness of the ship, it would be ideal for penetrating

Northfleet was the site of a shipyard producing naval gunboats. Here we see the launch of the *Pelter* in September 1854.

small creeks and rivers. The other three boats were to be called the *Pincher*, *Ranger* and *Snapper*. The first ship had been built in just nine weeks.

The shipyard must have been very successful, as along with the launch of the *Pelter*, after such a rapid construction, a commercial ship, the *Dom Pedro* was launched immediately afterwards.

GRAYS

Several training ships including the *Exmouth* and the *Goliath* were moored off Grays. The *Goliath* was operated by the Forest Gate Schools District. It provided training for boys from London's Poor Law authorities and helped them to join the Merchant or Royal Navy. This lasted until December 1875, when the ship caught fire; the assistant master Richard Wheeler and several of the pupils drowned.

A replacement was found in 1877 when the *Exmouth*, an old wooden ship built in 1854, which had been used during the Crimean War, was moored off Grays. *Exmouth* was managed by the Metropolitan Asylums Board.

GREENHITHE

In 1866, Lord Shaftesbury had the idea of using an old ship as a home for homeless boys in London. The idea that the ship could train boys to join the navy aroused the interest of the Admiralty. They provided a ship, the *Chichester*, which was moored off Greenhithe. The first boys arrived in December that year.

One of the first tasks was to teach the boys to swim but unfortunately a number of them drowned during training. A safer idea than using the river for swimming lessons led to a barge being tied up alongside and filled with water for use as a swimming pool.

One major problem relating to the boys from the ship was that the navy would not take recruits without a birth certificate. This rule was waived for boys from the *Chichester* as the majority had little idea of their origins.

An old map of the Thames from the West India Dock to Thurrock.

PURFLEET

The powder magazines at Purfleet were still in operation during the Napoleonic Wars and barracks were duly added to the site. There were also rifle ranges added in the fields stretching down to Rainham. When the magazine was overworked, powder was also kept in floating magazines in the river. These floating magazines were in operation during the Crimean War

There were worries about the safety at the magazine in 1864 after a large magazine explosion at Belvedere. The explosion was, it seems, caused by poor attention to safety at Hall & Sons and it was hoped that this would not occur at Purfleet. Especially as the amount of powder at Purfleet far surpassed that held at Belvedere.

What worried people more than the procedures at Purfleet, which had always been very good, was the transportation of gunpowder. There was little in the way of laws regulating this. There was no limit on the number of barrels of powder barges could carry or enforcement on using lights aboard them. It was believed that if any catastrophe did strike Purfleet, it would be because of an accident involving a barge.

A detachment of the 2nd Battalion, the Buffs at Purfleet, 1889. Although they have built a fine raft, I doubt if they crossed the Thames from Kent to Essex on it.

The soldiers at the barracks were not always welcomed by the local population. This was understandable when they did not always behave themselves. One night in February 1873 at 2 a.m., Mr Warren, the landlord of the Lennard Arms public house in Wennington, was awoken by two soldiers from Purfleet knocking on his door. They threatened to break open the door and kill the landlord if he did not let them in. They then broke open the door and helped themselves to a drink. The men then left. Mr Warren went to the barracks the next morning but because it was dark at the time of the offence, he could not identify the men responsible.

Also, in October that year, the *Cerberus*, an iron-plated turret ship, arrived at Purfleet to take on powder. The ship had been at Chatham for a year being refitted to sail to Australia. Once its powder was on board it went to Sheerness to take on coal.

There was also a near accident at the magazine when a ship carrying a dangerous cargo caught fire in the river near the base. The *Maria Lee*, under the command of Captain Richard Gilbert, left Plaistow Wharf carrying 200 barrels of naphtha, 119 barrels of petroleum, thirteen barrels of linseed oil and ninety barrels of pitch. It was on Sunday 20 October that there was a bad storm with thunder and lightning. The ship anchored at Long Reach and then set sail again, but during the night there was a loud explosion and the ship caught fire. The mate was at the helm and managed to get the ship across to the Kent shore, away from the magazine. The crew all escaped but the ship was completely destroyed by the fire.

Although there were powder ships moored off Purfleet in 1858, others followed later. These were the HMS *Conquistador* and the HMS *Mermaid* and were also used to hold powder.

Another development of the nineteenth century was the naval training ship. In 1859, Sir George Henry Chambers came up with the idea of caring for young boys who had got themselves into trouble. His idea was a naval training ship and the Admiralty offered him HMS *Cornwall* if he could raise £2,000. This was the origin of the School Ship Society.

The *Cornwall* was the first of the training ships and was moored off Purfleet. It had been built at Deptford in 1809. The first ship was replaced with another in 1868 but was still known as the *Cornwall*. It was used to take boys who had been in trouble with the courts. At first they would take no boy who had been sentenced to less than three years' detention, and only those aged between thirteen and fifteen who were fit and healthy.

In October 1871, the fathers of two of the boys on the ship were taken to court to force them to pay towards their sons' keep. William Waverley of Greenwich was earning 21*s* a week but had six other children to keep. George Bradshaw of Deptford earned 18*s* a week but had four other children. Both men claimed they could not afford to pay for their sons aboard the *Cornwall*. They were told that their neglect led their children to become thieves and were each ordered to pay 1*s* 6*d* per week.

BELVEDERE

In October 1864 two gunpowder magazines at Belvedere exploded killing nine people and wounding a number of others. The explosion was heard throughout London. The people of the capital thought at first that it was an earthquake. Although the explosion would seem to have caused some level of panic, thousands of people actually rushed down to Belvedere by train to see what had happened for themselves.

The explosions took place in the magazines belonging to John Hall & Sons and at a smaller magazine owned by Daye & Barker. Although the magazines were some distance from most local homes, there were some small cottages close by belonging to workers at the magazines. These were occupied George Rayner, storekeeper at Hall & Sons, and Walter Silva, storekeeper at Daye & Barker.

Hall & Sons had been producing gunpowder at the site for about fifty years, mainly for the government – they also had a large factory at Faversham.

PLUMPSTEAD

The marshes at Plumpstead were used for testing of guns weighing up to 80 and 100 tons. The noise of firing would echo over Shooter's Hill. There was a report on Plumpstead Marshes in the *Illustrated London News* of November 1854. It describes the area – 5 miles long and 1½ miles wide – as containing many ditches and stagnant water. Owing to this, the inhabitants of Woolwich were often seen as suffering from unnecessary sickness. The marshes were described as a hotbed of malaria. The Thames marshes were one of the last places in Britain where the disease existed.

WOOLWICH

On 28 July 1804, an Act of Parliament was passed to make compensation to the owners of certain lands in Woolwich and Charlton, which were to be used to promote the service of his majesty's ordnance. There was a meeting of the commissioners responsible for the purchase on 13 June 1804 at the Ship Tavern in Woolwich.

The aim of the meeting was to agree the value of the land with the owners. It is interesting to note that if the owners had been infants, lunatics, idiots, persons beyond the sea or otherwise incapable of acting for themselves, then the commissioners would have decided the price.

The dangers of the arsenal in Woolwich were shown in December 1830 while old rockets were being broken up in the blacksmith's shop. A spark set off an explosion, which destroyed the shop despite the walls being 3ft thick. No one was killed but one man was seriously injured.

Woolwich was still populated by large barracks during the nineteenth century and there was much less secrecy about military matters at this time. At the beginning of 1849, the strength of the army was published in the newspapers. It was composed of 7,093 regimental officers on full pay; 66 colonels, 266 lieutenant-colonels, 260 majors, 1,827 captains, 2,553 lieutenants, 1,227 second lieutenants, ensigns and

Barracks were rare in England before the Napoleonic Wars and those at Woolwich were among the earliest.

cornets, 490 staff officers, 185 surgeons, 249 assistant surgeons and 30 veterinary surgeons. There were 162,148 non-commissioned officers and other ranks. This total included 12,553 cavalry, 5,042 guards, 18,867 artillery, sappers and miners, 105,033 infantry of the line, 11,621 royal marines and marine artillery, and 8,520 in the colonial regiments.

There was reported to be a planned reduction in the size of the army of 10,000 men. This was to be done by reducing the size of a number of regiments. Those with 1,000 men would be reduced to 750. At the same time, there was a planned increase in the army of India. This was owing to a shortage of cavalry and the 12th Lancers and the Horse Guards were ready to leave for India. Of these totals, 3,000 men were based at the Woolwich Garrison. This included infantry and cavalry.

Woolwich was one of the sites where troops were loaded aboard ships for travel overseas. This often included horses for the cavalry and artillery. Although this was a difficult procedure in the mid-nineteenth century, the time taken to load a horse into a ship's hold was around two minutes. This was done by placing a canvas sling under the horse's stomach and lifting it into place using a block and tackle.

In the hold, the horses were kept in stalls and the canvas sling was left in place and fastened overhead with ropes. This helped to keep the horse on its feet. It also helped to support tired horses. The danger with horses on a ship was that they

The transport of horses abroad was a difficult task for the army and loading them on board ships provided entertainment for spectators at Woolwich.

The slings used to lift horses onboard ship were left in place to help keep the animals upright in the hold.

The guns built at Woolwich for the ship *Devastation* were so large – 38 tons – that they were facetiously given the nickname of 'the infants'. The size of the guns inspired so much interest that the Czar of Russia came to see them being made in June 1874 .

would suffer seasickness. As they are unable to vomit they go mad. If this happened they would be bled to death and thrown overboard.

On arrival at the destination, the horses would be unloaded as they were loaded if possible. Otherwise they were dropped overboard and allowed to find their own way ashore.

The arsenal and the dockyard were both busy providing for the protection of the country. The arsenal provided ammunition and weapons, and the shipyard built what were Britain's 'wooden walls' until metal ships replaced them. The arsenal was busy receiving goods returned from the Crimea in August 1856. The Chasseur military floating steam factory had been unloaded at the arsenal while a decision was made as to its future. The storehouses at the Arsenal were described as glutted with materials being returned from the east.

The last warship built there was the *Thalia* in 1869 but the yard was very busy up until this time. In August 1856 the paddlewheel steam vessel *Medusa* was in the inner basin of the dockyard, having undergone extensive repairs. The screw steamship *Rattler* was in the dry dock and found to be riddled with dry rot.

The production of weapons such as the Harvey Torpedo was often open to the view of the public at the arsenal. The idea of necessary secrecy was to come much later.

Queen Victoria visited the wounded from the Boer War at the Herbert Hospital, Woolwich, in March 1900.

There was also an Admiralty breaking yard, where old wooden ships of the line met their end. Regarding industry, Siemens began production there in a small factory in 1863.

There was also a naval training ship, the *Warspite*, moored there until moved on to Greenhithe and then Grays. It had been used to train boys for the Navy from 1876. In 1877 the arsenal began to manufacture a different kinds of torpedo. The Whitehead Torpedo had been the subject of a discussion in Parliament. There was a demonstration of the Whitehead variety by a new torpedo vessel, the *Lightning*.

The Harvey Torpedo was also built there and was used for different purposes, such as when one ship was chasing another. Rather than the pursuing ship being the aggressor, the Harvey could be fired by the ship that was being chased. The torpedo was set afloat in a box and then left to hit the oncoming pursuing ship. The process of manufacture was open to public inspection at the arsenal and could be viewed by visitors.

BOW CREEK

Bow Creek was the site of Thames Ironworks shipyard. This had previously been owned by Mr Mare of Mare & Ditchburn at Blackwall. In 1860 the Ironworks launched the *Warrior*, the first ironclad battleship. They built several ships for a number of navies across the world, right up to the beginning of the twentieth century. The last ship they built was the *Thunderer* in 1910.

Shipyards such as Thames Ironworks must have profited from the Naval Defence Act of 1889. It looked as though the British Navy may have to support Italy against France, while also having to keep an eye on the Russians. Having to fight on two fronts led to the act, which originated the Two Power Standard. This meant that the British Navy should always exceed the next two largest naval powers in strength.

Thames Ironworks went out of business in the early twentieth century but left a lasting heritage in the shape of its football team, which later became West Ham United.

Further up the River Lea was the site of an ancient abbey, which was occupied by something very different in the nineteenth century. An armament factory stood on the site, which produced military rockets. The rockets were designed by Sir William Congreve and had been used at Waterloo, despite the fact that Wellington was not impressed by them.

The River Lea was used to carry gunpowder down to the Thames from the mills at Waltham Abbey, despite the dangers involved in passing the built-up area around Bow Bridge. It was these unregulated powder barges that were a cause of worry over gunpowder safety.

Thames Ironworks was responsible for producing a number of large ironclad warships on the Thames.

Rockets were first experienced by the British fighting in India. William Congreve was the son of another Sir William Congreve, Controller of the Royal Laboratory at Woolwich and of the Royal Gunpowder Mills. In 1814 the younger Congreve also became Controller of the Royal Gunpowder Mills. He invented warheads for rockets which, despite not being very accurate, were much easier to transport than large artillery pieces.

The rockets were used by the British in Boulogne Harbour in 1806 with some success. Congreve opened the factory at Bow to make the rockets. It covered 14 acres and was close to the Three Mills site between 1821 and 1866. After this, the factory moved to Dagenham for a short period. Although the rockets were made at Bow, the propellant was supplied from the Royal Gunpowder Mills at Waltham Abbey.

BLACKWALL

At Blackwall was a shipyard called Green, Wigrams & Greens. The *Penny Magazine* of 1841 printed an article explaining how the shipyard worked, which would have been similar to most other yards along the river at that time. The yard stretched for between a quarter and a third of a mile along the riverbank and had built warships during the Commonwealth period and were still doing so in the nineteenth century.

The article on a day at a shipyard showed how the process of building a ship evolved from the raw materials to the finished article, as though building a model.

The yard was shown full of piles of timber still in the form of cut trees. There were a number of ships at several stages of construction, not one ship being built at a time, as well as older ships awaiting repair. The complete process of building a ship was carried on in the yard, from planning to shaping rough wood into the parts of the ship to its final launch. The process was described in detail, which involved making several different parts in wood and in metal.

Another of the shipbuilding firms of the nineteenth century at Blackwall was Mare & Ditchburns. In 1853 they built the *Himalaya*, the largest merchant ship of the time. It was later converted to a troopship for the Crimean War.

GREENWICH

The pensioners from the Royal Naval Hospital must have been a common sight around this area. Greenwich was the point of arrival for many people visiting the country. When Queen Caroline landed there in 1795, she asked if all Englishmen had an arm or a leg missing because of all the disabled men wandering the area. The hospital had many naval connections, one of which was a model frigate in the grounds for the use of the boys from the hospital school to familiarise themselves with ships.

Greenwich became the centre of attention for the world in 1805. The Loyal Greenwich Volunteers, the River Fencibles and numerous members of the public gathered outside the hospital grounds. They were waiting for the arrival of one of England's greatest heroes, Lord Nelson, who was to return from Trafalgar. Unfortunately, it was his body that was being carried along the Thames, saluted by the guns at Tilbury and Gravesend.

The body never arrived until well after midnight on Christmas Eve, carried on board Commissioner Grey's yacht. Nelson lay in state at the hospital until 8 January, when he was carried upriver by barge for his funeral.

The men at the seamen's hospital were quite visible, apart from their disabilities, as they had uniforms. This was before the navy themselves had a proper uniform. In another connection with Nelson, his captain from Trafalgar, Thomas Hardy, by then Sir Thomas, became the governor at the hospital in 1830. The hospital was in use until 1865 when the pensioners were offered incentives to return to their own homes.

An old map of the Thames from the Tower to Greenwich.

MILLWALL

Fire was an enemy that seemed to strike quite often at the shipyards on the banks of the Thames and it is interesting to see how large conflagrations were dealt with in the mid-nineteenth century. This was shown when the steam shipbuilders, Scott, Russell & Company's yard caught fire in September 1853.

The company had its own fire engine but this could not cope and the public fire engines mistakenly thought that the fire was in the dockyard at Deptford and

Hulks were a common site on the Thames during the Napoleonic Wars and were used to hold prisoners of war. They were also used to hold convicts.

Fire was always a danger at the Thames shipyards and could cause great damage despite the nearby location of an unlimited water supply from the river to fight potential blazes.

crossed the river. They then had to go back across London Bridge. There was also a floating steam fire engine that was for the protection of the dockyard at Deptford, which also came to help. Although not able to put out the fire for some time, the fire brigade managed to stop it spreading to other yards in the area. Two new steamships about to be launched were damaged, as were most of the premises.

The fire did not put Scott, Russell & Company out of business – by the middle of 1854, they were launching a large Australian steam ship called the *Pacific*. Although by this time the screwship seemed to be taking over from paddle-wheel steamers, this was not entirely true, as the *Pacific* was a paddle steamer.

Another shipbuilder at Millwall was turning out ships in 1856. Samuda's Works employed 800 men who made an iron steam-gun battery. The *Thunderbolt* was the first all-iron vessel built for fighting.

DEPTFORD

Deptford dockyard dated from Tudor times but played a large part in the defence of the country during the Napoleonic Wars. Along with other Thames naval yards, it quickly prepared ships for sea.

In February 1849, there was an Admiralty circular published, which intended to reduce expenditure and increase productivity in the dockyards. The number of shipwrights was to be reduced to 3,500 with a corresponding reduction in other workers. This was to be done by keeping the younger, fitter men, while disposing of the older ones, who were no longer able to do the job. The number of apprentices was to be reduced and working hours would be seven hours and ten minutes per day in winter and nine hours ten minutes in summer.

Also based at Deptford at the time was the *Dreadnought*, a ninety-eight-gun warship that had fought at Trafalgar and had captured a Spanish Triple-Decker. The ship's guns had by then been removed and changed for beds, for it was used as a seamen's hospital.

There was very little secrecy about the strength of the naval forces and the *Illustrated London News* published details of the strength of the navy in November 1853. It included 545 ships of war which carried from ten to 180 guns. There were 118 ships engaged in harbour duty and fifty revenue vessels. Of the total ships, 180 were armed steamers.

The force was described as the largest fleet of any maritime power and was run by 40–45,000 able seamen, 4,000 able lads and 12,000 Royal Marines. The Marines were divided into 102 companies shared between Chatham with twenty-five and Woolwich with twenty-five. Each dockyard also had its own volunteer force

ROTHERHITHE

Although there were rules forbidding the manufacture of gunpowder close to London dating back to the eighteenth century, in the mid-nineteenth century, Rotherhithe was the site of a rocket factory owned by a Mr Hale and his son. In April 1853, the Hales were arrested and charged with keeping a stock of gunpowder, which was more than the permitted amount, within 3 miles of London. There was, however, more to the case than at first seemed.

The Hale's rocket factory at Rotherhithe was found to be breaking the law by having more than the permitted amount of gunpowder close to London. The objectives of the rockets were also a problem.

Also involved was a Hungarian named Louis Kossuth. Kossuth had been Governor of Hungary and, in 1848, had proclaimed independence for the state. This led to a war with Austria and Russia, in which Hungary was defeated while Kossuth fled. He eventually found himself in England and was suspected of levying a war against Austria from England. This led to problems between Britain and Hungary with British subjects being refused entry into Hungary.

During the trial of the Hales, it was claimed that an ex-member of the Hungarian artillery had been given a job at the rocket factory under the orders of Kossuth. It was suspected that the rockets might have been for use against Austria. The Hales claimed that the rockets were exported to a number of countries but could produce no documentary evidence for this.

Kossuth's house was searched at the time of the raid on the factory. Lord Palmerston refused to state in Parliament that Kossuth had nothing to do with the production of the weapons. The rockets were taken to the Royal Arsenal at Woolwich for safekeeping. The Hales were committed to prison to await trial.

LONDON

When the moat at the Tower of London was drained in 1843 it would seem that the use of the castle as a defensive structure was at an end. There was still, however, a garrison at the Tower. In June 1854 it was the turn of the Essex Rifles Regiment of Militia commanded by Lord Jocelyn. They were the first militia regiment to provide the garrison at the Tower. They had travelled to Shoreditch from Colchester by railway.

Although no longer a defensive structure, by the mid-nineteenth century the Tower of London still had a garrison. This was the turn of the Essex militia.

A large crowd watched the 700 men march to the Tower from the station. They were dressed in green and carried a rifle and short sword that could be used as a bayonet. The regiment were also reviewed in Hyde Park. They returned to the Tower by marching to Hungerford Bridge from where they took steamers to the Tower.

Later that year, in October to be precise, there were celebrations at the Tower when guns were fired to celebrate the victory in the Crimean War. Strangely, the guns announcing victory were fired at six o'clock in the morning. The weapons were based on the new Saluting Battery between the Chapel and Waterloo barracks.

CHELSEA

One of the best-known military establishments on the Thames is the Chelsea Hospital. The hospital provided a similar service for old soldiers as the Naval Hospital at Greenwich did for sailors. The *Illustrated London News* of 26 May 1849 described

Military balls were lavish affairs in the nineteenth century. This ball was at the Commercial Hall, Chelsea, in 1849. The hall was decorated with swords, helmets and insignia and the band of the 1st Regiment of Life Guards played all evening. The ball ended at 6 a.m., after a rendition of the National Anthem.

The Governor of the Royal Hospital at Chelsea during the middle of the nineteenth century was Sir Edward Paget, a veteran of the Napoleonic Wars.

the hospital as extending 800ft in length along the river – a noble monument of nations. The gardens at the hospital were opened to the public in 1833 after a long period of closure. The hospital and its soldiers should be seen according to the *ILN*, especially the chapel and hall with its war standards and paintings.

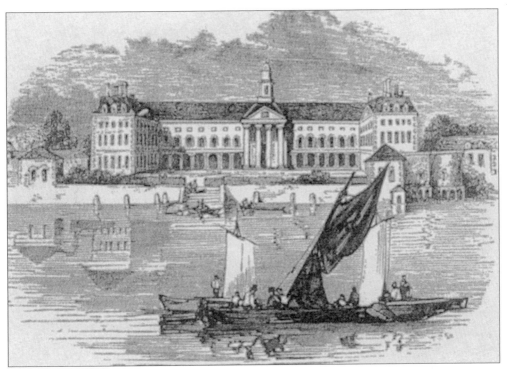

A view of the Chelsea Hospital from the River Thames.

CHISWICK

Although it seems a strange place for a shipbuilding yard now, in 1864 John Thorneycroft opened a yard at Church Wharf. In the late nineteenth century, the company built a torpedo boat, HMS *Speedy*. The boat had a new design of steam engine, which was safer and faster than what had been built before. HMS *Speedy* was sunk by a mine in 1914.

The company went on to build torpedo gunboats such as HMS *Daring* and HMS *Decoy*. As the ships the company built got bigger, sailing them down the Thames became more difficult because of low bridges. By the early twentieth century the company had moved to Southampton.

HOUNSLOW

During the eighteenth century, a gunpowder mill was opened on the bank of the River Crane. The mill itself was much older and had been used for various other items before turning to gunpowder production.

As with other gunpowder mills, there were several explosions, some causing fatal injuries during the lifetime of the mill. One of the worst was when, in 1796, the mills were blown up which completely destroyed the building killing three people. The mill was rebuilt and continued in production until after the First World War.

The queen reviews the families of reservists at Windsor during the Boer War.

The accidents continued and in April 1859 there was another large explosion. The uncertainty of gunpowder production was well described in *The Times*, when it stated that gunpowder could be rammed by gentle taps 9,999 times with impunity before a child drops a rod on it causing the loss of numerous lives.

The 1859 explosion had taken place in the pressing house. Although the press was still standing in the centre of the building, the pressing house itself had vanished. The press was described as acting as a large piece of ordnance, destroying everything around it while leaving itself intact.

The danger of such explosions had led to the question being asked whether Hounslow was the correct place for the mill. The fact that there were eighty men applying for the jobs of the eight men who died in the explosion showed that jobs were more important to most men than safety. Especially at *2s 2d* a day in wages. The fact that the mill went on producing powder until well after the First World War showed that weapons were also more important than safety.

KINGSTON

During the nineteenth century, barracks were built in Kingston in 1874/5 on land owned by Lord Liverpool at Park Farm. There had been earlier militia barracks at Fairfield. The militia barracks do not, however, seem to have been big enough for in July 1876 the 1st Regiment Surrey Militia had to hire a camping and drill ground next to the barracks. They also hired the volunteer rifle range and cottages for the staff sergeants.

An old map showing the river from Kingston to Chelsea.

The Thames was in constant use as a means of training the troops during the nineteenth century. Here, the officers of the Horse Guards and Life Guards swim their horses across the Thames somewhere in Berkshire.

Troops from the Chobham encampment of July 1853 practise on a pontoon across Virginia Water. They later repeated the exercise across the Thames with fatal results.

The presence of the army in Kingston was not a new event, however. As an important crossing point of the river there had been soldiers stationed in the area for much of the recent past.

The new barracks were designed by a Major Siddon of the Royal Engineers. They were very modern for the time. While the 70th Foot were serving in India, recruits for the regiment were trained at Kingston.

CHERTSEY

In July 1853 a large military camp was set up at Chobham. In command was Lieutenant-General Lord Seaton, who, at seventy-seven, was a veteran of the Napoleonic Wars. The camp included cavalry, horse artillery and infantry.

These summer camps were the tourist attractions of their day and large crowds would flock to see the sham battles that took place as training exercises. Not only members of the public attended, but Members of Parliament and also Prince Lucien Bonaparte. Use was made of the Thames as a means of training in how to cross a river.

At one point Lord Seaton marched his division to Runnymede and built a pontoon bridge across to Magna Carta Island where they fought a staged battle.

The use of pontoons had already been practised on Virginia Water. The exercise did lead to some real deaths, for on the way back across the bridge, a cannon being drawn by six horses fell into the river. The men and four of the horses were rescued but the other two horses drowned.

ETON

Eton is the site of probably one of the best-known schools in the country, but what has that to do with defending the river? Maybe there was an indirect effect on the defence of the whole country. The Duke of Wellington supposedly said that the Battle of Waterloo was won on the playing fields of Eton. The number of names on the school's war memorials would seem to point to an influence on many of the battles fought by the British throughout history. There were more than 1,500 deaths of old Etonians in the First World War.

The Chobham camp had many distinguished visitors, including Prince Lucien Bonaparte.

A veteran of the Napoleonic Wars, seventy-seven-year-old Lieutenant-General Lord Seaton was the commander of the troops at Chobham camp.

HENLEY

Henley church contains a slab set into the floor marking the resting place of the Frenchman General Dumouriez. He died at Turville Park, the home of John Bowring. Dumouriez is believed to have been the mastermind behind the Duke of Wellington's strategy in the Peninsular War. The general was an enemy of Napoleon and was so important to the British government that they gave him a pension of £1,200 a year. It is thought that it was also his plans that were used to win the Battle of Vittoria.

A portrait of a noble-looking soldier in late nineteenth-century Reading.

An old map showing the Thames from Eton to Sunbury.

FOUR

The First World War

The period leading up to the First World War resulted in another spell of re-arming many of the defences that already existed along the Thames. Although secrecy in relation to defence was not as strict as it was to be in later conflicts, there were some attempts at security. When Sir G. Parker, the MP for Gravesend, asked in Parliament in July 1907 whether all the minefields in the Thames had been deactivated, he did not receive an answer. He also asked if the recently mounted new guns had been removed from Hope Battery, Cliffe Fort, New Tavern Fort and Tilbury Fort. He also wanted to know if the Brennan Torpedoes

The early twentieth century was the heyday of the volunteer force. Here we see an advertisement from the *Thames Illustrated Magazine*. The Yeomanry spent many weekends at displays at local fêtes or in war games around the countryside.

The wreck of a zeppelin believed to be in the Thames Estuary.

had been abandoned at Cliffe Fort. Parker did receive an answer when Mr Haldene replied that it was not expedient in the interests of defence to answer his questions.

The First World War also led to the expansion of munitions factories in the areas bordering the Thames. This had always been a common practice, especially with gunpowder mills, but legislation had led to these only being built below Blackwall. The danger of munitions factories in highly populated areas was illustrated during the war, with probably the most devastating damage ever caused by explosions in these factories.

Many of the guns mounted at the Thames forts were moved at the outbreak of war. There seemed to be an attempt to move the defences, especially the heavier guns, closer to the mouth of the river.

The majority of the defences updated for the war were concentrated below London. The attacks that came were from the air and reached as far up the river as the capital. Above London, however, the situation was different. Although there was a shortage of actual defensive structures, the towns lining the river played their part in the war effort in other ways.

Munitions factories were in operation in a number of places along the river above London. There were even boatyards producing torpedo boats. Troops were also billeted in many of the towns, both in private houses and in the many new army camps that grew all around the country.

A captured German submarine being towed up the Thames.

SHOEBURYNESS

By the end of the nineteenth century, the artillery had been divided into two sections, the Royal Garrison Artillery and the Royal Field Artillery. Shoebury was mainly involved in the garrison side of the artillery and concerned mostly with naval weapons.

Men from Shoebury were posted to other areas to help defend important sites. While those concerned with artillery may have been moving away, other troops such as the Border Regiment arrived to help protect the site from sabotage and invasion.

In 1917 a large fire began to burn at the ranges, which led to widespread evacuation. Many of those evacuated were put up at the Kursaal in Southend. The fire destroyed a great deal of ammunition that had been bound for the front.

SHEERNESS

In June 1900 there was a distinguished visitor to Queensborough. Francis Reginald Wingate was the Sirdar, or Commander-in-Chief, of the Egyptian Army. He had taken over the position from Lord Kitchener when he left for South Africa. Wingate had arrived at Queensborough on a two-day visit to see Queen Victoria and was accompanied by an Arabian servant who had previously been with Kitchener.

Unfortunately, the Sirdar was suffering from influenza when he arrived and it was suspected that he might have had diphtheria. He was therefore confined to his ship for several days before he could finally meet the queen.

The pre-war period was an important time for the development of aircraft and the area along the Thames was the site of a number of early airfields. One of these was at Eastchurch and Mr Cecil Grace made a number of flights from the airfield in a Short Wright biplane across the Isle of Sheppey.

One of these flights, in May 1910, involved a tour over Sheerness and the warships in the Medway. Mr Grace was reportedly loudly cheered by the crew of the cruiser *Natal* and other ships in the port. The highest altitude he achieved was 1,500ft at a top speed of 70mph.

There were plenty of opportunities to practice for the defence of the Thames before the First World War began. On 8 June 1911 at 2 a.m., a raiding party attacked the troops defending Sheerness. They had arrived on a late train from London, which seemed a strange means of travelling to an attack. What the local people must have thought of an outbreak of firing at that time can only be imagined. The defenders must have been more prepared for an attack from the sea rather than on land.

Troops were based all along the Thames as this postcard of the Rifle Brigade shows. This was intended to reassure the public.

There was also an attack from the sea to support the land forces. This was at Harty Ferry about 10 miles from Sheerness. The attacking force was discovered by cavalry, sent out by those defending the town.

The manoeuvres at Sheerness seemed to be attracting unwelcome attention in 1912. An aircraft was heard flying over the town by several people. The weather was too stormy for an aeroplane, so it was thought to have been a zeppelin. The news was taken up by the press and it was reported that German airships were training over the town at night.

This led to action by the First Sea Lord, Winston Churchill, and naval planes were based around the coast – this was despite the fact that there were hardly any aircraft capable of carrying guns at the time.

Another threat was seen to come from enemy aliens. In August 1914, Franz Heinrich Losel, a German photographer, was arrested with a camera on the sea wall near Sheerness naval harbour and was charged under the Official Secrets Act, though no evidence was presented. Losel was then rearrested under the new Aliens Act. As he was to be removed under the act, he asked the court what he could do about the home that he owned. The house was 300yds from the Ravelin Battery at Sheerness and had often been damaged during the practice firing of the guns. The court was unable to give him any advice in the matter.

Sheerness Dockyard was as busy during the war as it had been in all previous conflicts.

There was not only a threat to Sheerness from the air but also from the sea. This was not just from enemy ships. The British battleship *Bulwark* exploded while loading ammunition close to the town in 1914. Only a few of the crew of 700 survived the accident.

Even land-based defences were to cause a problem for the town's inhabitants. There were several new batteries built, as well as improvements to existing defences. Shells from one of the new batteries fell on the town during gun practice in 1918. It was at first thought that the town was under attack, but luckily the shells did not contain explosives.

THE MEDWAY

Although not actually part of the Thames, the Medway is one of the most heavily defended tributaries of the Thames. Its strong naval links with the dockyard at Chatham has led to a number of fatal disasters.

HMS *Princess Irene* had been a passenger liner for Canadian Pacific but was taken over by the navy during the First World War. The ship then exploded in Saltpan Reach and sank. Another ship alongside the *Princess Irene* also sank after the explosion. This was a nineteenth-century French frigate that had been captured and renamed HMS *Forte*. It was being used to hold coal when it went down. The site of the *Princess Irene* is still marked with a buoy.

On land, new defences were added in the early twentieth century. A boom was built across the river from Grain to Burntwick Island. There was a battery at each end of the boom with two 12-pounder quick-fire guns. The boom was to stop torpedo boats from entering the river.

The buoy marks the wreck of the *Princess Irene*, which sank during the First World War.

CANVEY ISLAND

The late nineteenth century saw the arrival of an explosives factory at Canvey Island. Kynoch & Company was very busy during the Boer War and opened the factory to support its factories in other parts of the country. The works were built on the site of Borley Farm at Shell Haven. The site was not the best for building on, owing to its marshy nature.

A variety of explosives were made at the factory, along with bullets and most of the buildings were set well apart from each other in case of an explosion. The First World War led to great expansion of the factory and included a large increase in the number of women employed there.

The complex was guarded by the military to keep out any suspicious characters. This did little, however, to protect it from air raids. The works suffered from being on the banks of the river, which made it easy to find for enemy air attacks and was finally the cause of its demise.

There was an interesting idea put forward for its protection from air raids by a member of the Sportsman's Battalion, who were based at Hornchurch. The members of the battalion had been digging trenches for coastal protection at Leigh. John Chessire wrote a letter to his wife suggesting that German prisoners be held at the site to deter bombers from killing their own countrymen.

COALHOUSE FORT

The fort, as a defensive structure, was as good as obsolete by the time the war began, but it was still put to use. The Royal Garrison Artillery was stationed there to man the guns that were to defend against air- rather than water-based attacks. There were also searchlights manned by the London Electrical Engineers. They were used to fire on the zeppelins that often used the Thames as a guide into London. A minefield was laid in the river and an old ship, the *Champion*, was moored in the river by the fort. Boats from the *Champion* checked ships travelling upriver.

The soldiers at Coalhouse Fort attempted to rebuild the tower at the nearby church before they were stopped by officers. This plaque was, however, set into the church wall.

The fort became a training depot for soldiers who lived in the barracks, in tents and in nearby homes. Some of the men from the fort had the idea of rebuilding the nearby church tower, allegedly destroyed during the Dutch attack in the seventeenth century. Unfortunately, they were ordered to stop before it was complete. However, the tower does contain a memorial to the men from the fort who died in the war, as well as to General Gordon.

TILBURY

The guns at Tilbury Fort during the war were fired in anger and were successful. They damaged a zeppelin, the L15 that came down in the sea close to the *Kentish Knock* lightship. As well as being armed with anti-aircraft guns, the fort became a supply base and was also used to house troops destined for the trenches in France.

The importance of Tilbury during the war was highlighted by the fact that the ferry was no longer seen as an adequate means of crossing the river. The Port of London Authority was responsible for making a floating bridge of seventy lighters and three miles of timber across the river to Gravesend. The bridge was used to move both mounted troops and infantry across the river. The centre of the bridge could be removed to allow ships to pass through.

A zeppelin caught in searchlights. Anti-aircraft guns were positioned at many points along the river.

This section of the Suffolk Royal Garrison Artillery were based at Gravesend during the war.

PURFLEET

The camp at Purfleet was to be used for the training of men in the First World War, so it was useful that the travel to the camp had been improved. Railway sidings had been built near the camp and a new signal-box installed called Purfleet Rifle Range Box.

By September 1914 there were 10,000 recruits for the new army on the marshes next to the rifle ranges at Purfleet. At the time it was fortunate that the land was still dry as they were living in a city of tents. The whole area was covered in men exercising and drilling.

At the time they had no uniforms or rifles so they were parading in civilian dress. They were also short of officers and so the Dean of Ontario, who was the chaplain of the men, was acting as a drill instructor. His qualification for this was previous service as an adjutant in the Canadian 14th regiment.

In November 1915 the Civil Service Rifles arrived at what they called Rainham Musketry Camp. It was so cold on the marshes that accurate firing was impossible. They were also not very complimentary about the village, saying that it only took five minutes to see all of it.

A naval training ship, the *Cornwall*, was moored off Purfleet and was manned by young boys. There was a scandal concerning the boys in 1903 when twenty of the ship's inhabitants caught typhoid. It was then found that blankets on board, bought

As well as serving at other stations along the river, the London Electrical Engineers were also based at Purfleet and issued this card.

The Thames had a number of naval training ships, such as this one. Many were for boys who had been in trouble with the police or were homeless.

from a dealer, had come from South Africa and had not been disinfected; it was from these that the disease had spread.

It seems that life on the ship was not safe for the boys, for in September 1915 a cutter from the ship holding twenty-six boys and one officer was hit by a government tug. The boys were aged between thirteen and eighteen; sixteen of them drowned including the officer.

The officer was named Fred Lane and was an ex-naval petty officer. Although several boats were launched from the *Cornwall* and the shore, it was only possible to save ten of the boat's occupants.

An inquest was held at the Royal Hotel and Samuel Robinson, the schoolmaster on the *Cornwall*, identified the bodies. The inquest was attended by the commander of the ship, Captain Steele. The commander of the tug, William Blackmore, was also present. Blackmore was a company sergeant major of the Royal Engineers based at Dover. He was also a master mariner by trade and said that the cutter had changed direction and cut across in front of the tug. In 1928, after nearly seventy years at Purfleet, the ship was moved downriver to Denton near Gravesend. The increased industrialisation of Purfleet meant that the shore where the *Cornwall* had been moored was to be used to hold oil tanks.

DAGENHAM

Although the battleship *Thunderer* was built at the Thames Ironworks at Bow Creek in 1910, there was nowhere big enough for it to berth. It was decided that it would be fitted out at Dagenham Dock. Work was carried out at Samuel Williams & Sons. The ship arrived in February 1911, along with members of the Thames Ironworks employees and a 150-ton crane. The *Thunderer* was unlucky as building it bankrupted the Thames Ironworks. The ship also seemed to carry on its bad luck and was sunk at the Battle of Jutland.

Dagenham Dock also played another part in the war materials of the First World War. Many of the stores and vehicles returning from France after the war came back to Dagenham. The heavy traffic had an adverse affect on the road leading to the dock and Chequers Lane was upgraded.

WOOLWICH

There was a lot of public unrest in the years before the First World War. As a result, in 1911 there were large bodies of troops stationed in several parts of London, including Woolwich. Far from there being a patriotic atmosphere among the population, it was feared that the troops might be needed to control the public during any disorder. Although public feeling may have changed during the war, afterwards there was a return to bad feeling among the working class.

During the war, Woolwich became a very busy area with the high number of munitions workers there. A worker could earn a significant £5 per week at the local munitions works.

Then there was a change back to pre-war conditions as the end of the war led to what would have been a tragedy at the arsenal. It was planned to lay off a number

"ARETHUSA" JACK APPEALS FOR HELP

The "ARETHUSA" and "CHICHESTER" TRAINING SHIPS

prepare poor British Boys of good character for the Royal Navy and Mercantile Marine.

SUBSCRIPTIONS AND DONATIONS WILL BE THANKFULLY RECEIVED.

THE NATIONAL REFUGES FOR HOMELESS AND DESTITUTE CHILDREN.

(Incorporated 1904.)

Patrons: THEIR MAJESTIES THE KING & THE QUEEN.
President: THE EARL OF JERSEY, G.C.B.
London Office: 164 SHAFTESBURY AVENUE, W.C.
Joint Secretaries: H. BRISTOW WALLEN and HENRY G. COPELAND.

Running training ships was expensive as this appeal for help from the *Boy's Own* paper shows.

of the workers who were no longer needed in peacetime. A deputation went to present a petition to the Prime Minister, asking him to postpone the discharge of workers and allow them to undertake other work. Unfortunately, with thousands of men returning from the trenches, it was not just munitions workers who found themselves without a job.

The Royal Military Academy at Woolwich was responsible for training officers for the Royal Artillery and the Royal Engineers. It was known as the Shop and had an entry exam, which included papers on English, Maths and French or German. One of the questions in the final exam was based on where to site trenches for infantry.

One of the best-known names and faces of the First World War had begun his military career at the Shop. Horatio Herbert Kitchener is best remembered for his figure pointing out from a poster, which attempted to get men to enlist for the army. In February 1868 he entered the Royal Military Academy and passed out in December 1870, qualified to take up a commission in the Royal Engineers as a lieutenant in January 1871.

SILVERTOWN

The area around Silvertown and Bow Creek was a favoured spot for building chemical works in the late nineteenth century. There were less regulations from the local councils at the time and the smell from these factories made living in the area very unpleasant. One of the chemical works in Silvertown was Bruner Mond, which opened in 1893 at Crescent Wharf. The factory closed down in 1912.

The factory reopened in 1915 for war production purifying TNT. This was despite the fact that the area was heavily populated. On Friday 19 January 1917, a fire broke out in the factory. The fact that everyone living in the area knew what the factory produced led to a rapid evacuation of the area by many residents and workers from nearby factories.

There was estimated to be around 50 tons of TNT in the factory, much of it already loaded onto rail wagons. The factory exploded, destroying not only Bruner Mond, but also several other factories in the area, the nearby fire station and several streets of houses. The explosion was reportedly heard 100 miles away and is believed to have been the biggest-ever explosion in London.

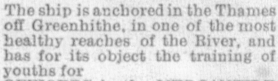
Some of the training ships were more up-market than those which only took boys in trouble. The *Worcester* advertised for cadets in the *Boy's Own Paper* in the years coming up to the war.

Seventy-three people died and more than 400 were injured. This included firemen who had been fighting the fire, despite knowing the danger. The damage was to cost £2.5 million, which was an enormous amount in those days.

Owing to wartime censorship, the event was not reported in the newspapers until three days after it happened and, even then, details of what occurred were very sparse. The explosion was also quickly forgotten and any mention of it in the press seemed to have been frowned upon.

LONDON

The declaration of war led to an outbreak of fear over enemy aliens who were at large in the country. The press played a full part in encouraging the panic, which eventually led to internment for the majority of what were seen as enemy aliens. As early as August 1914, a warning was issued to gunsmiths in London that it was an offence to sells arms or ammunition to an enemy alien.

Although the blackout in the Second World War is common knowledge, it is not as well-known that there was also a partial blackout imposed during the First World War. In September 1914, the Commissioner of Police of London issued a notice saying that in order to make it more difficult for German airships to identify parts of London, it was requested that arc lights, sky signs and illuminated fascias should be switched off.

The searchlights shining up into the sky is a scene that most would associate with the Second World War, but this card dates from the First World War.

The Hotel Cecil and Somerset House were used as up-market recruitment and training centres for the New Citizen Army during the First World War.

The effect of turning off the lights was to be examined by a naval airship, which was to fly over the city for three or four days. As well as the official blackout, many shops also dimmed their lights and streetlamps also remained unlit. Even lights in trams were turned off.

When the air raids began, there was a ready-made source of safety in the underground stations of the capital. This was used as another way of turning public opinion against enemy aliens. The *Morning Post* reported how swarms of aliens pushed women and children aside to be first into the safety of the tunnels. They were described as acting like 'brutish beasts'.

London was one of the busiest centres of enlistment for the new army. The recruitment figures for the ten days at the end of August and early September 1914 in London were:

August		September	
26	1,725	1	4,600
27	1,650	2	4,500
28	1,780	3	3,600
29	1,800	4	4,028
30	1,928		
31	1,620		

HMS *Buzzard* was a naval training sloop moored at Blackfriars. In 1911 it changed its name to HMS *President*.

Although the vast majority of the men enlisting were from the lower classes and went straight into the ranks of either established or new regiments, there were also other forms of enlisting men. At the outbreak of war, the army was entirely made up of volunteers, so new schemes to encourage enlistment were welcome.

Sir Henry Rawlinson came up with the idea that if men could serve with others from their own locality, then they would be more willing to volunteer. The Pals battalions were duly formed and on the first day of the Battle of the Somme many towns and villages lost almost all their young men to the German machine guns in a few vicious hours.

The Pals battalions were raised by private money and were mainly from the working-class areas in the North. There were also privately raised battalions in London but these were often seen as more up-market. One example was the Sportsman's Battalion. Raised by a woman, Mrs Cunliffe Owen, a relative of royalty, their recruiting office was the Hotel Cecil on the bank of the Thames. It was once the largest hotel in Europe. Entry to the battalion was restricted to sportsmen, although this parameter was later lowered to ex-public school boys. Of course, all public school boys were seen as sportsmen. Another special privilege that the sportsmen had was that men up to the age of forty-five could serve in the ranks, whereas in other battalions the age limit was thirty-five.

Bomb damage occurred in London during the First World War, although not on the same scale as the Second World War. This photograph shows bomb damage on the embankment from a raid on 4/5 September 1917.

A programme from the Thames Pageant of August 1919 to celebrate victory in the war. A huge number of craft took part in the parade.

Below: An anti-submarine boat taking part in the pageant. There were a number of boats like this one that had hidden guns, which were run out when a submarine surfaced near them.

There were also several volunteer rifle units that dated back to the mid-nineteenth century who were formed into fighting units in the war. One of these was the Civil Service Rifles, whose headquarters were at Somerset House. The large open square in the centre of the building was used to drill the men. When the unit first came together, the men were living at home and travelling to Somerset House daily.

CHISWICK

One of the best-known aircraft engine makers of the First World War was based in Chiswick. Gwynnes was situated on the banks of the Thames and had taken over the premises of the Thorneycroft Shipbuilders after they left the area.

Much of the work carried out during the war was performed by women. One of these workers, Miss Joan Williams, wrote a memoir of her time at the factory entitled, *A Munitions Workers Career at Messrs Gwynnes, Chiswick, 1915–1919*. Joan came from a very upper-class background but found working on a lathe in the factory exciting. She discovered that her fellow workers were quite willing to make friends with their high-class workmate.

Although munitions factories had excellent first-aid facilities, which were not the norm at factories in those times, there were still dangers. Women in munitions factories were given the nickname 'canaries' as the TNT they dealt with turned their skin yellow. There were more than 400 female deaths during the war due to exposure to TNT. Although there was no TNT used at Gwynnes, there were other dangers and Joan had to have the grit from using the machines scraped out of her eyes.

As well as the factories producing war goods at Chiswick, there was a large influx of soldiers. At the outbreak of war, 5,000 men and officers of various regiments were billeted in private homes in the town.

A captured submarine on the Thames. After the war, more than a hundred surrendered German submarines were sailed into Harwich.

Although there was a great rush of volunteers in the first few months of the war, there were concerns about enough men being found for the trenches of France. At a meeting in Chiswick in November 1914, Lord Selbourne called on the government to make up its mind on separation allowances, pensions and widows pensions payable to recruits. They also needed to state how many men were wanted, when they were needed and, if enough volunteers were not found, then whether conscription must be used.

It was not only the men of Chiswick who took part in war work. The senior boys at Chiswick trade school used their Whitsun holiday in May 1915 to help with the manufacture of armaments. They went to work at the Westminster Engineering Company. While the boys worked in munitions, the school staff all joined the army.

BRENTFORD

There were calls from many quarters for professional football to be cancelled during the war. This would then allow all players to join the army. Many did, but some London newspapers were almost fanatical about their campaigns to stop football. A meeting of the members of the Football League in Manchester in December 1914 decided to carry on playing.

The league meeting was followed by the eleven professional London clubs, including Brentford, holding their own meeting. Although critical of the press campaign, they agreed to shut their grounds if racecourses, golf courses, music halls and cinemas were also closed.

January 1915 saw an unusual petition from the vicar and churchwardens of St George's church in Brentford. They wanted the authority to fix a box to the wall with a glass front to exhibit a prayer book. The petition was granted. The book had previously been the property of drummer George Charles Edward Court of the 1st Middlesex Regiment. It had been given to him by his fiancée when he left for the front. She asked him to carry it in his left breast pocket close to his heart. Finding it uncomfortable there he transferred it to his trouser pocket while taking part in the Battle of the Marne.

A shell exploded close to him and the shrapnel killed six men and wounded fourteen. Drummer Court was unhurt, but after the battle, he found a hole in his trouser pocket and a tear in the cover of the bible. At the bottom of the bag containing the prayer book, was a bullet.

RICHMOND

There were a number of army training camps based around the Richmond area in 1914. Much of their training took place in Richmond Park and there was even a Richmond Park camp where dances were held and attended by local nurses, as well as soldiers. One of the most important forms of training could not take place in the park, however, and had to be done elsewhere. The soldiers were not allowed to dig trenches in the park in case it spoiled the area. When one considers how many open spaces in other areas were used for this purpose, it seems to show that even in war the better-off areas still didn't have to put up with as much bother as the rest.

One unit training in Richmond early in the war were the Civil Service Rifles, but due to a shortage of NCOs, training was very basic. As they had no weapons, there was very little they could do apart from drill with wooden guns. Field kitchens were set up to feed the men training there. The men also lived in tents in the park until billets were found in local homes.

In 1916 a strange sight must have greeted the locals around the park when No. 2 Balloon Training School took up residence. Observation balloons were used to spot targets for the artillery. Each group consisted of two trucks and around ninety men. While the balloon filled with hydrogen was raised up to 3,000ft, a circle of machine guns would be set up around it for protection.

One other thing that occurred in Richmond during the war was rugby, played at Richmond's ground between different branches of the forces. On 12 December 1914, the Canadians based in London played the Public Schools Battalion who were quartered in East Surrey. The PSB was a kind of up-market Pals battalion, whose members all came from public schools and universities. There were even plans at one point to have school companies such as an Eton company and a Rugby company.

Because of the high level of players in both the Canadian forces and the PSB, the match could have been classed as an international. As it was, the game drew a large crowd with all proceeds going to the Belgium Relief Fund.

There was also a game in March 1915 when the Royal Army Medical Corps played and beat the Honourable Artillery Company. Proceeds from the 3,000-strong crowd went to the Tobacco Fund for soldiers and sailors.

Richmond was also the site of military hospitals, including a South African Red Cross Hospital at Richmond Park. A number of the patients were men from the famous South African action at Delville Wood.

There was also another hospital called Latchmere House Military Hospital for Mental Cases on Ham Common. Shell shock was only recognised late in the First World War. Unfortunately, this was only after many men suffering from it had been shot as cowards. By the end of the war, men who had been mentally scarred by the conflict were more sympathetically cared for.

In December 1918, however, there was a tragedy at the hospital when Lieutenant Sidney Hume RAF, a patient at the hospital, was arrested for shooting private Robert Aldridge RAMC. The superintendent at the hospital, Major Norman Oliver, said that Hume was suffering from delusions. He believed that he had been hypnotised by German doctors while he was a prisoner of war, and that the same thing was afoot at the hospital.

KINGSTON

The barracks in Kingston dated back to the nineteenth century but still played a part in the First World War. One of the uses the barracks was put to may now not be seen as something to be proud of. Conscientious objectors were not always treated with respect at that time and the barracks were used as a place to persecute them. One eighteen-year-old was told by the tribunal that he was too young to have a conscience, but not to fight in the war.

The police took him from his home to Kingston Barracks where they tried to force him to become a soldier. Once there, he still refused to follow orders and was court martialled and sent to prison for six months' hard labour. In reality, most conscientious objectors spent the majority of the war in prison.

In September 1917 the wounded men at the new barracks hospital and at the Kingston Infirmary were given a treat by Lady Wolseley. She had bought 210lb of grapes from the great vine at Hampton Court and distributed them to the wounded at Kingston and other areas.

Men from the barracks at Kingston took part in an unusual event after the war in 1920. A film studio was opened in Surbiton at Regent House, a large mansion with extensive grounds. The studio was responsible for making several films about the First World War. Men from the East Surrey Regiment based at Kingston were often used as extras in the films.

WINDSOR

One of the guests at Windsor Castle in 1905 was to have a great influence on the British army during the First World War. Douglas Haig was staying at the castle for Ascot Races and was popular with the king. While at the castle he met his future wife, Dorothy Vivian, who was one of the queen's ladies-in-waiting. Haig was to oversee many of the battles in the war that proved costly in losses of British servicemen.

The First World War had little effect on everyday life on the upper reaches of the Thames, apart from an increase in the number of soldiers based in many of the riverside towns, such as Windsor.

In August 1914 the panic over enemy aliens being German spies led to the arrest of a man in Windsor. Edward Newman claimed to be an Australian on a trip to England. He was charged with being a suspected person after he was found acting suspiciously by the Thames near Windsor Castle waterworks. He also had a camera in his possession. It was found that the address he gave in Gillingham had only been occupied by him for a few hours.

During the war, a camp was set up at Smiths Lawn in Windsor Great Park. It was occupied by the Canadian Forestry Corps, who had their headquarters there. The corps was formed after an appeal from Britain for men to carry out lumbering work. This included building barracks and hospitals, clearing sites for airfields and supplying timber for trenches.

In April 1916, Princess Victoria of Schleswig-Holstein opened a YMCA hut at the camp. She was not the only royal person to visit the Canadians. The previous day the king and queen had passed through. Also at the opening ceremony were Colonel Claude Willoughby, deputy ranger of Windsor Great Park; the Revd Moore, Chaplain of the Great Park, and numerous other officers.

The YMCA hut had been built by the Forestry Corps in seven days. It was a large building fitted with electric lights, a coffee bar and billiard room. The hut was named the Princess Victoria Canadian Recreation Hut. Lieutenant-Colonel Penhorwood, the CO of the corps, thanked the princess and said that though they were from a distant land they had made many friends in England.

The Canadians had around seventy different operating centres in Britain. The Forestry Corps did not only work in this country but they often worked at the frontline in France while under fire from the enemy.

TAPLOW

Cliveden is a large estate on the Thames, which was owned by the Astor family. During the war, a Canadian Red Cross hospital was built in the grounds under the patronage of the Duchess of Connaught. There was an Italian garden on the estate, which had been laid out in 1902. The garden was adapted for use as a cemetery for those who died at the hospital. There are forty-two people buried in the cemetery and twenty-eight of these are Canadians. There are also the graves of Australians, New Zealanders and some British. They are not all men, as two nursing sisters are also buried there. There were also a number of Americans whose bodies were removed after the war and taken home.

The hospital continued to be used after the war as a Canadian general hospital and there were further burials in the cemetery during the Second World War. Cliveden is one of only three war cemeteries in Britain, the others being Cannock Chase and the American Cemetery at Cambridge.

MAIDENHEAD

Preparations for the coming conflict were underway well before the war began. The 3rd London Field Ambulances spent a weekend taking part in practices and exercises in April 1914 in Maidenhead. This was part of a wider military ambulance practice throughout London.

The 3rd Rifle Battalion crossing the Thames in August 1909.

During the war, thousands of soldiers came to the Maidenhead area for training. A club was set up in a school by the Revd Mr Way, from the Jubilee Community Church, for the soldiers. A soldiers' prayer meeting was also held on Tuesday evenings.

Maidenhead also became involved with escaped German prisoners during the war. In April 1915 two German officers escaped from Llansannan Camp near Denbigh. The search for them was mainly concentrated in Wales, but two men answering their descriptions were seen in Maidenhead and stayed at the White Horse Hotel. They claimed to be Belgian refugees on their way to London. They left and were never seen again.

In February the following year, another two German officers were tried by a military court at Philberds in Maidenhead. Lieutenant Otto Thelen of the German Army Flying Corps and Lieutenant Hans Kehhack of the German Navy were charged with attempting to escape from Holyport prison camp where they had been sent after escaping from the camp at Donnington Hall. The two men were sentenced to nine months' detention at the military detention barracks at Chelmsford in Essex. They were taken from the court to Chelmsford by car with an armed escort.

MARLOW

There was a large military camp at Marlow in August 1913. The 4th Infantry Brigade was camped on Marlow Common, near Bovington Green. They were joined by the Scots Guards and the Irish Guards. It seems that the area was used as a regular camp, for in June 1915, the Grenadier Guards arrived at Bovington Green Camp. A number of these left for France in October that year. There were a number of trenches dug in the area by some of the men from the camp as practice for what they would be expecting in France.

HENLEY

One of the important aspects of the army camps in England was partly organised from Henley during the war. Lieutenant-Colonel Leonard Noble lived in the area and was vice-chairman of the YMCA camp committee. Mr Noble wrote to *The Times* in August 1914, explaining how the experience they had gained in territorial camps was being used to provide YMCA services in the new camps springing up around the country.

The association provided marquees or rented rooms and halls where off-duty soldiers were welcome. Free writing materials were provided, as the very common YMCA letterheads of correspondence from the forces during the war shows. They

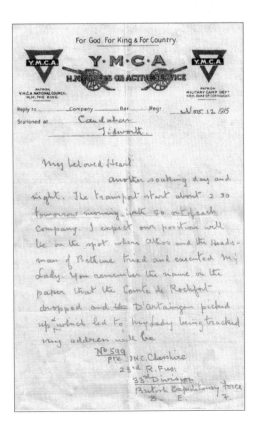

A letter written on the famous YMCA headed notepaper that was supplied free to many of the troops during the war.

also provided cheap refreshments along with entertainment. This often included concerts performed either by the soldiers themselves or by locals in the vicinity of the camp.

Lieutenant-Colonel Noble's letter of 21 August mentioned 230 centres opened by the YMCA in camps. A further letter from Noble, a few weeks later, mentioned that this number had risen to 500. This was all possible because of voluntary workers and donations of cash.

There was an interesting mention of Henley in a letter from the front in January 1915. Reports had begun to filter back of the Christmas Day truce between the British and German troops at the front. An officer in the rifle brigade said that the Boche trenches were lit up like the Thames on Henley Regatta night. There were Christmas trees burning along the parapet.

Henley, like other towns along the Thames, had soldiers billeted in private homes. One of theses soldiers unfortunately never made it to the front. Sapper William Lea was billeted in Henley and had been on a route march to Hurley in May 1915. On his way back he had visited the Black Boy Inn with friends from his regiment; for some reason he left them on the way back to Henley.

He was later found lying in the road at 4.40 a.m. suffering from terrible scalp wounds. He had been run over by a car and dragged along by it. Strangely, there was a fox terrier guarding Lea, who stopped the man who found him, William Kitchen, approaching him. After being taken to a local public house, the East Arms at Hurley, he later died. Car parts were found spread along the road and Lea's cap was found 300yds away.

READING

When war broke out there were two regular battalions of the Royal Berkshire Regiment. There was also a third battalion, which was a reserve and training unit. The depot of the Royal Berkshires was at Brock Barracks, Oxford Road, Reading. The barracks were named after General Brock who had fought in Canada and died at Queenston on 13 October 1812.

When war broke out, the commander of the barracks was Major F.W. Foley. The major later went to serve in France with the fifth battalion until wounded in December 1915. The depot was used to issue uniforms and equipment to the men who were called up from the reserve. Most of these went to make up the numbers of the first and second battalions.

The first battalion fought at Mons, Marne and Aisne. At the Battle of Aisne, the battalion spent thirty-two days engaged in the battle, all but five of these in the trenches. A report in *The Times* in November 1914 stated that this example should encourage all able-bodied men from Berkshire to enlist.

The newspaper also printed a copy of an order from Lieutenant-Colonel M.D. Graham, the commanding officer of the first battalion. The order was put on display at Brock Barracks. The notice read: 'The commanding officer has been directed by the commanding officer of the 2nd division to convey to the battalion the very high appreciation of their attack of 24th October 1914 and the determined manner with which they held their ground.'

This soldier sent the photograph of himself taken in Reading in April 1918 to his mother. It was simply signed 'Alfred'.

OXFORD

Oxford, being a university city, played a different part in the war than many other towns along the Thames. One example was when a Peace Manifesto was published in early August 1914 by university professors who enjoyed the friendship of German colleagues. They believed that it was a mistake that a country so like our own should be an enemy in wartime. One of the signatories was the principal of an Oxford college.

There was, of course, an opposing view within the colleges, which was put to use by the propaganda machine. There were calls that those involved in teaching should put their skills to use by promoting the causes for the war. This would enlighten the people and encourage enlistment in the forces. Oxford was seen to be leading the way.

Similar to the debate raging over whether professional sport should be postponed so that the players could enlist, many believed that universities should have been shut during the war to allow the students to join up. The universities themselves were of course against this view. They argued that many students were exempt from service and that others may be able to defer service until they had completed their degrees.

The colleges did, of course, aid the war effort in a great many ways. Some Oxford colleges were used as barracks for local territorial units, the cricket pitches were used as drill grounds and an exam school became a hospital with 500 beds.

A Christmas and New Year greeting card from the Oxfordshire & Buckinghamshire Light Infantry.

There was already involvement in the forces by many students and the commanding officer of the Oxford University Officer Training Corps informed both graduates and undergraduates who had served in the OTC that he would be pleased to receive their names for commissions in the forces. The qualification for this was to have served in the OTC and be between the ages of nineteen-and-a-half and twenty-five. They were to apply at 9 Alfred Street, Oxford.

In September 1914 *The Times* printed a list of the young men from Oxford colleges who had applied for commissions:

Keble	85
New	83
Magdalen	82
Christ Church	77
Balliol	69
Oriel	69
Brasenose	62
University	61
Exeter	57
Trinity	57
Merton	47
Hertford	47
Queens	43
Worcester	37
Corpus Christi	36
Wadham	29
Lincoln	28
Jesus	27
Pembroke	27
Non-Collegiates	12
St Edmunds Hall	8
All Souls	3
Marcon's Hall	1

Although the numbers vary greatly, it should be remembered that All Souls only had four undergraduates, so the percentage applying was in fact very high. As the total number of students at Oxford was around 3,000 (and many of these were foreigners), the total number of applicants for commissions was very high.

Oxford also played a part in early aviation at Port Meadow, which was used for flying before the war began. During the war, canvas hangars were built along with some huts and tents erected for the men. There were a number of fatal crashes at the field and there are ten men from the airfield buried in Wolvercote cemetery. One of these men is an American, William Smith Ely. He was a member of the aviation section of the US Signal Corps. Aircraft were initially considered to be solely of use as a means of reconnaissance, which was why the origins of the

CAPTAIN

OXFORD LIGHT INFANTRY, MARCHING ORDER.

A captain in the Oxford Light Infantry wearing the colourful uniform which was swapped for khaki during the war.

US Army Air Force was as part of the Signals Corps. Smith Ely came to Britain in July 1917, then went to France. He returned to Britain and became a squadron leader at Port Meadow. In January 1918 he was a passenger in a plane that crashed, killing him and the pilot.

At one point, American airmen were billeted in Queen's College while training in the area, for which they were paid $100 a month.

In October 1914, the king left Buckingham Palace and travelled by car to Paddington station. From there he travelled by special train to Goring. He was accompanied by General Sir Ian Hamilton, Commander of the Central District. The king was to inspect the mounted division who were training at Goring.

A description in the press said that no finer place for the evolution of mounted troops could be conceived than the rolling hills that overlook the loveliest reaches of the Thames.

The division was paraded on the Fair Mile near Churn Camp. His Majesty was mounted on his own horse for the inspection at which there was a display of cavalry protecting the horse artillery.

LECHLADE

There were often conflicting views about matters relating to the war. There were calls for increased production from farms to help feed the nation and ease the food shortage. Unfortunately, some saw the idea of allowing young men to remain on farms working and not joining up as wrong. A man named George Dewar wrote to *The Times* in June 1918 to report that in the previous six months he had been travelling in country areas and had seen numerous strapping young men in their twenties and thirties not in khaki. A specific case was mentioned at Lechlade Market, where he saw a crowd of young men, mainly farmers' sons. There were up to twenty of them. Although men were needed in France, not one of them had ever served in the forces.

Dewar went on to argue that there has been much said about the lack of labour on farms causing problems (*see* Cirencester). However, women and German prisoners could have carried out farm work.

CIRENCESTER

There were a number of soldiers based in Cirencester during the war. The 40th Brigade were assembled on Salisbury Plain and moved to Cirencester in September 1914. The South Wales Borderers were sent to the town in December 1914 and were billeted in local houses.

Although there seemed to have been plenty of soldiers in the area, there was a shortage of farm labourers. This seems to have been the opposite of the situation in Lechlade. In Cirencester, so many farm labourers had enlisted that local farmers could not cope. There were forty farms in the area with no tenants, as the farmers could not carry on without more help.

There was another connection between farming and the war in Cirencester. A professor, John Wrightson, had put forward a scheme for settling disabled and time-served men from the forces on the land. This would give the men and their families an opportunity to be self-supporting while also producing more food.

The idea was supported by the Board of Agriculture and the Duke of Portland who was to become vice-president of the society. This was also supported by the principal of the Royal Agricultural College in Cirencester, J.R. Ainsworth Davis, who agreed to be on the committee.

The idea of soldiers taking over smallholdings after the war was quite a popular one. In some places, a number of Canadian soldiers decided to stay in Britain and many built their own log cabins on small plots of land, which they then farmed. The problem with the scheme was that so many soldiers attempted it, that it was hard to find a market for their produce. Most of the smallholdings were based on such small

The Citadel and park gates with cannon either side in Cirencester.

Another view of the Citadel, now described as the Armoury, with a soldier on guard at the door, but the cannon are missing.

plots that they were never really viable and most of the men quickly went out of business.

It seems that men from Cirencester were involved in a number of wartime schemes that were not always successful. A letter to *The Times* in May 1917 from the Civil Medical Officer at the Cirencester Voluntary Aid Hospital, Howard Marshall, was very critical of government policy in relation to civilian doctors.

It seems that civilian doctors had, at the outbreak of war, offered their services to voluntary aid hospitals. As doctors were paid for their services at that time this meant they were losing money by spending their time working with wounded men for nothing. There was, it seems, no attempt by the War Office to do anything about this problem.

It turned out that this was not quite the case. Mr Marshall had discovered that the War Office had decided to pay 3*d* a day per bed for hospitals taking patients from overseas and 2*d* a day per bed for men transferred from other hospitals. This rule had been in force since June 1915. The payments were, however, only paid on application and Mr Marshall claimed that the availability of the payments had, in fact, been concealed from doctors on official instructions. The only way they could get the payment, if they did know about it, was to agree to conditions that they were not allowed to see.

Even if a doctor should find out about the payments and claim them, the actual amount payable for a year based on a ninety-bed hospital would be £135. Mr Marshall pointed out that this was less than the average annual salary of a typist employed at the War Office.

FIVE

The Second World War to Today

T he Thames played an important part in the Second World War, not only for the home population. The river was a very useful guide for German aircraft to find their way up to London and drop their bombs. There were attempts to restrict this by using the blackout, but of course the river could be easily seen on moonlit nights.

In early August 1939, the steam launch *Sherbourne* sailed along the river during the blackout. On board were naval personnel and the harbour master, who were checking the effectiveness of sailing at night without illumination. This was a nerve-

A barrage balloon over the Thames during the Second World War.

wracking journey as neither the *Sherbourne* or any of the other craft on the river were showing any lights. The only lights were the dim glow on ships working through the night at some docks. Many of the important works on the river such as Woolwich Arsenal, Barking power station and the Ford works at Dagenham were in complete darkness.

There were, of course, several groups who played their part in the war by using the river. One of these was the Upper Thames Patrol. This was a waterborne Home Guard unit who used launches to patrol the river. Their job, if an invasion took place, was to blow up the bridges across the river. The Upper Thames Patrol was not the only river-based Home Guard unit (*see* Gravesend). There were also many land-based units all along the banks of the river from the sea to its source.

ESTUARY

During the Second World War, a number of Maunsell Forts were built in the Thames Estuary. These towers were designed by Guy Maunsell, who had begun his war-related designs with submersible lookout towers that were never actually built.

The first of the non-submersible Maunsell towers to be built were four naval towers which were constructed in the Holloway Brothers' Yard on the Thames at Gravesend in early 1941. The first fort, completed in February 1942, was Rough's Tower, and was actually positioned off Harwich. That was followed by Sunk Head Tower a few months later, also close to Harwich.

The earliest of the naval forts positioned in the Thames Estuary was Tongue Sands, off Margate, in June 1942. It was followed by Knock John off Foulness in July 1942. These were followed by three army forts in the Thames with the Nore Fort in July 1943, Red Sand in September 1943 and Shivering Sands in December 1943.

Shivering Sands Fort, one of the Maunsell Sea Forts on the Thames. (*Frank Turner*)

The Bofors Tower in the Shivering Sands Fort. The platforms on either side were where the guns were positioned. *(Frank Turner)*

The forts' crews spent six weeks on duty before being relieved. This was later reduced to four weeks. The size of the crews was increased with the arrival of the doodlebug attacks.

The towers were rarely used after the Second World War ended until the Korean War broke out in 1950, and the escalation of the Cold War led to the refurbishment of the towers. After that threat was over, a number of the towers were dismantled, though some remain. The towers later found another use as pirate radio stations until the government shut them down.

SHOEBURYNESS

There was a great expansion in the number of men based at Shoeburyness during the war. They were accommodated in wooden huts that were erected on the sports field. The beach was mined and lined with barbed wire to keep out anyone attempting to land from the water.

Shoebury Barracks is now a private housing estate, which incorporates many of the original buildings along with newly built homes.

The wire was also supposed to keep out anyone from the land as well. Unfortunately this was not completely successful and a young boy got under the wire and set off a mine. A soldier attempted to get the injured boy out, set off a mine himself and died.

SHEERNESS

Between the wars, naval manoeuvres were still carried out on the Thames. In August 1925, at 10 p.m., the guns at Shoeburyness were fired on the artillery ranges. The defences at Sheerness were manned and spotlights were used to watch for an attack by torpedo boats. A destroyer, HMS *Stork*, was sighted and was fired upon with blank ammunition from Garrison Point.

Guns at the Ravelin Battery at Sheerness were also tested for the first time since the end of the First World War. The local population were warned of the barrage by an air raid siren. Those living nearby knew to open their windows, as the vibrations from the guns could shatter the glass in closed windows.

The defences at Sheerness were updated at the beginning of the war. More modern guns were added to older defences, including anti-aircraft guns. Radar was

Garrison Point Fort dates back to the mid-nineteenth century, but has been updated both above and below ground since.

also introduced. As was the case in the First World War, the whole of the Isle of Sheppey became a restricted area and a pass was needed to enter or leave the island.

The Thames off Sheerness was full of ships in June 1944, preparing for the invasion of France. Not all the ships from the Thames managed to get across the Channel, however. One of them, an American ship loaded with munitions, sank.

The USS *Richard Montgomery* had arrived from America in late 1944 loaded with ammunition. The ship was directed to a position off Sheerness to wait until it was ready to sail to France. The name of the ship was perhaps not the most suitable for one involved in the allied war effort. It was named after an eighteenth-century Irish soldier who had fought the British in Canada.

While waiting in the river, the ship ran aground. It was decided to remove the cargo to enable the ship to be refloated. Before this could be completed, however, the ship broke apart.

Although some of the munitions were removed, most were left aboard and are still there today. Although a regular check is kept on the ship, there is a danger of the craft exploding, which could cause an enormous amount of damage. The wreck is well marked by buoys and the masts can be clearly seen above the surface.

The masts of the USS *Richard Montgomery*, which sank during the Second World War and still contains large amounts of explosives.

The dockyard at Sheerness still has a number of old defences along the shoreline.

After the war, the Royal Navy Auxiliary Service was based at Sheerness and the Emergency Port Control for the Medway was based at Garrison Point. This was to control shipping in the event of a nuclear war. Part of the nineteenth-century magazine under the fort was converted into a nuclear bunker.

QUEENSBOROUGH

There was a large flotilla of minesweepers based at Queensborough during the war. The squadron was known as Wildfire III. HMS *Tudno* was moored in the River Medway at Queensborough and was the depot ship of the Nore Minesweeping Division. Surviving members of the squadron hold a parade every September in the Riverside Gardens to commemorate the base.

MEDWAY

The war proved to be lifeline for the dockyard at Chatham, which had been facing a difficult time in the 1930s. New ships needed to be built and older ships updated. Many of the tunnels under the area were ready-made safe bases for control and radio stations.

Preparations for attacks from enemy forces were well underway before war was declared. In April 1939, 1,600 troops took part in an air raid drill at Chatham. A warning of attack was received at Kitchener Barracks and forwarded to other forces stationed at Chatham, Rochester, Gillingham, Shornemead Fort and the Isle of Grain. The attack was carried out with fireworks representing bombs. Steel helmets and gas masks were compulsory.

Many of the old defences were updated, which included the mounting of anti-aircraft guns. Many of the defensive positions along the Thames were manned by the Home Guard.

The gates to the historic Chatham Dockyard. It is now open to the public.

Apart from the obvious part played in the war by the dockyard and the numerous barracks and bases, one of the largest works battalions of the Home Guard, the 31st Dockyard Battalion, Kent Home Guard, were also based there.

The battalion quickly saw action against enemy aircraft and one man, Private Blakey, was killed in December 1940. They were, at the time, the 14th Battalion but then later became the 31st.

During an exercise against the Royal Navy, the Home Guard came up with an idea that was sure to win the game but would not have had the same results against an invasion force. Large numbers of naval personnel were being brought in as prisoners during the war game. The answer to how well the Home Guard were doing in the game was answered when it was found that they were using grenades made from cloth bags full of whiting. If hit, the sailors faced hours of kit cleaning, so they readily surrendered.

SOUTHEND

One of the most useful peacetime structures at Southend was the pier. It actually played a big part in the war effort and was known as HMS *Leigh*. The pier railway was in constant use, carrying men to their ships and the wounded from ships back to

Although Southend Pier survived the war almost unscathed, there have been a number of fires since, which have caused severe damage. This photograph taken in 2007 shows the results of the most recent.

The steamers at the end of Southend Pier were used for pleasure trips. In the war, however, they carried evacuees and troops from the beaches of Dunkirk.

shore. The ships entering the Thames were watched by men on the end of the pier after it was taken over by the navy in 1939. The structure was machine-gunned from the air on several occasions.

During the pre-war period, the pier at Southend was the calling point for steamers from London taking day-trippers to the coast and beyond. Many of these steamers also played a part in the war effort; they picked up evacuees from places along the river such as Tilbury and Dagenham and took them round the coast to safer sites like Lowestoft. Later in the war, some of the steamers were at Dunkirk helping to take the soldiers off the beaches and bring them home. For some, it was their final trip. Many of the pleasure boats were then taken over by the navy and continued in service as anti-aircraft boats in their normal home of the Thames.

ISLE OF GRAIN

The acts of bravery that have been performed during the whole of the war must have been beyond estimation. One, however, was recognised as the bravest deed of 1940 and it was not in one of the better-known theatres of war – it took place at the Isle of Grain.

On 30 January 1940, leading seaman Harry Lucas and stoker Thomas Phillips RN were in a motor boat that capsized in the rough water 300yds from Grain Tower. Phillips was not a strong swimmer.

Grain Tower from the river. Although originally similar to a Martello Tower, later adaptations have altered its appearance.

Lucas gave Phillips his lifebelt and an empty oil drum to help him stay afloat. Lucas stayed with Phillips, swimming slowly in front of him and encouraging him to follow. On reaching the shore, Lucas ran across the fields that were deep in snow, badly cutting his bare feet on barbed wire before reaching Grain Tower. Although collapsing from exhaustion, he insisted that help be sent to Phillips who was found unconscious on the beach.

Lucas received the Stanhope Gold Medal for Naval Seamen from the Royal Humane Society for the bravest deed of the year. He was recommended by the Admiralty for the honour.

COALHOUSE FORT

A number of the old forts on the Thames were reused during the Second World War. One of these was Coalhouse Fort. It was used as an anti-aircraft base and was also armed with two 5.5in guns taken off HMS *Hood*.

A special operation was set up at the fort to help deal with magnetic mines. Equipment in the river checked the polarity of ships as they passed the fort on their way out to sea. An electric current was passed through the ships, which lessened the

An unusual two-storey Second World War pillbox at Coalhouse Fort.

chance of their being damaged by magnetic mines. The equipment at the fort was checked to see if this had been carried out correctly, otherwise the ships were sent back to have the process repeated.

A minefield was set up in the river close to the fort and was controlled by a two-storey pillbox situated between the fort and the river.

TILBURY

The fort at Tilbury had been neglected since the 1920s but was brought back into use when the Second World War began. It was manned by the Home Guard. The gun operations room controlling all the anti-aircraft guns on the Thames and the Medway was based in the chapel at the fort until 1940.

The old barracks in the fort were destroyed by bombing. Other bombs were exploded in the grounds around the fort, but these had been brought from other areas for this purpose.

During the build-up to D-Day, the area around the fort and docks became a park for military vehicles. Many of the men accompanying the vehicles never left them, not even to sleep. There was even a tented camp within the docks for military personnel. The vehicles were loaded on to ships in the river that then sailed towards the sea and across to Normandy for the D-Day landings.

The interior of the chapel at Tilbury Fort. During the Second World War it was used as a control centre for all the anti-aircraft guns on the Thames and the Medway.

GRAVESEND

It may seem strange to include the 24th County of London Battalion of the Home Guard under Gravesend, but this will become clear with further explanation. The 24th was a unique unit. It had permission from the Admiralty for its members to wear leading seamen anchors beneath the battalion numbers.

The battalion was formed in 1942 and was mainly made up of lightermen and tug-owners and their crews. It was similar to the old fencible units of the Napoleonic Wars. Some officers and NCOs of the 6th and 14th COL riverside units transferred to the 24th.

A number of naval vessels were moored in the Thames during the Coronation of Elizabeth II. British Rail were offering river trips to see them.

One of the large guns at New Tavern Fort, which dates back to the pre-First World War times.

A Bofors gun at New Tavern Fort. These were used on the Maunsell Forts in the Thames Estuary during the war.

The 24th was formed much later than most Home Guard units but it may have taken this long for the powers that be to realise how important the Thames was. The number of barges and boats on the river would have been an ideal means of crossing the river by an invasion force and it was these craft that needed guarding.

Unlike other Home Guard units where the men lived in the area that they served, the 24th had members from along the river both above and below London. Training therefore took place at numerous points between Gravesend and Brentford. This meant that the 24th covered much of the river not patrolled by the Upper Thames group.

The 24th had a problem that did not apply to other units. When trying to find winter training sites, their presence was often resented by local groups who did not want them interfering in their areas. As with other units, the 24th formed guards of honour. One of these was for the Prime Minister when he travelled by river from Westminster to Greenwich.

GRAYS

If you believe the popular propaganda about the war, then very little crime took place during the conflict. However, war obviously created the opportunity for new types of crime to be committed. There are known reports of men being charged with stealing Anderson Shelters which would have been a crime confined to wartime. Another such crime was committed by a man from Grays in September 1939.

A carpenter from Grays stole 1,400 empty sandbags, the property of London County Council, which he sold for £13. He was a foreman with a firm of contractors carrying out sandbagging work for the council. The man's employer said he had been working long hours on important ARP work and asked the magistrate not to send him to prison, as he would be more use working than in prison. The cost of the bags was deducted from his wages.

In 1948 the seventy-four gun *Worcester*, built in 1839, was moored off Grays as a training ship. It had previously been moored at Greenhithe as part of the Thames Nautical College. The ballast in the ship shifted and the ship sunk.

Men from HMS *Worcester* naval training college at Ingress Abbey, Greenhithe, July 1944.

PURFLEET

It was not only the barracks at Purfleet that played a part in the war. One of the largest companies in the area was Thames Board Mills, which is sited on the bank of the Thames close to the barracks. During the war, they turned their production to war-related items such as shell and mortar containers, prisoner of war boxes and engine gaskets, along with numerous others.

Production continued throughout the war, despite heavy air raids and damage to the factory with thirty-eight bombs falling on the works during the war. The workers would often file into the shelters while a raid took place and then get straight back to work at the all-clear.

As well as keeping production going, a number of the employees joined the Thames Mills Home Guard. They took part in manning anti-aircraft batteries to protect the factories in the area. A special unit was formed and trained on Bofors guns in 1943 to deal with the expected counter-attacks after D-Day, which never materialised.

The barracks at Purfleet were used to house troops and were often used in training. The rifle ranges attached to the site that were close to the Thames were used for bombing practice and for training by both regular and Home Guard units.

The ranges were later used as a gathering area

The clock tower that marked the entrance to the barracks at Purfleet. Part of the original wall is also still in place.

during preparations for D-Day. The men could board ships on the Thames without travelling very far.

One of the few remaining buildings from the barracks at Purfleet. This now stands in the centre of the housing estate that covers the site. It was once used as a chapel.

DAGENHAM

The docks at Dagenham played a part in numerous aspects of the war. Thames steamers that had carried day-trippers from London to Southend now took evacuees from Dagenham to safer homes around the coastline of Suffolk.

Tugs from the docks also played their part in the evacuation of Dunkirk. These were the *Prince*, the *Princess* and the *Duke*. The *Duke* was the only one that reached Dunkirk and picked up men from a number of lifeboats. They got back to England with their men.

Dagenham may not have been an important military or defensive site, but it is a prime example of how it was not only the forces that played a part in the war effort. A number of factories that had been in operation before the war producing run-of-the-mill items were turned over to much more important war work.

One of these factories was involved in an incident that rivalled the storyline of any wartime spy thriller. A man named George Patchett was working at an arms factory in Czechoslovakia. Winston Churchill himself was involved in smuggling Patchett out of the country before the Germans invaded. Patchett was then installed in the Sterling factory in Dagenham, where he designed a machine gun to replace the obsolete Lanchester model that the factory had been producing.

The May & Baker chemical works was just up the road from Sterling and large quantities of the factory's products were taken away and stored in safer areas of

A number of defences were built in Dagenham during the war. This pillbox marks the end of a line of anti-tank obstacles that run along the railway line by what was the old May & Baker chemical works.

the country. To keep production going, a number of underground bunkers were built for the workers and a direct telephone link was set up with the nearby RAF Hornchurch.

The Ford Motor Company was in a precarious position on the bank of the Thames, because the river was used by German pilots to find their way to London. Because of this, the government was at first loath to use the factory to produce war vehicles. This soon changed and the factory produced thousands of military vehicles and engines for aircraft.

BARKING

One of the first dogfights of the Second World War took place over this area and became known as the Battle of Barking Creek. Unfortunately, it turned out to be an error when Spitfires from Hornchurch mistakenly attacked Hurricanes from North Weald. Two Hurricanes were shot down, and one pilot, Pilot Officer M.L. Hutton-Harrop was the first British airman killed in the Second World War.

WOOLWICH

Preparations for the war were not without problems for those close to the river. In August 1939 a barrage balloon collapsed and dropped on a house in Woodland Terrace, Charlton, and took off part of the gutter.

While the upper Thames may have had its share of pleasure craft still working, the river below London was often concerned with much more serious work. One new arrival on the river, however, was the waterbus. With the difficulty of travel in the

The Arsenal gates at Woolwich. The Arsenal was always obviously much busier during conflicts than in peacetime.

capital where bombs often disrupted the running of trains and buses, the use of the river was a safer alternative.

The Ministry of Transport began the service for those travelling to work between Woolwich and Westminster Bridge. There were several stops on the way, and the return fare was 9*d.* The passengers also included a fair share of those in uniform, as well as workers. The boats were usually small steamers that had previously been used for pleasure trips on the upper Thames. The larger steamers that had travelled between the Tower and the sea had mainly been drafted into war service of a more serious nature.

Vandalism is thought of as a modern phenomenon and memories of the war tend to concentrate on how everyone pulled together and did their best for the war effort. It seems strange then, that there were cases of vandalism against those most important items for public protection – air raid shelters. What is even more surprising was a case at Woolwich Arsenal on 3 March 1944.

The event involved seven young boys who were all employed at the arsenal. One of them was eighteen and the others were all sixteen. The charges were that during the lunch hour, the boys pulled the tarpaulin covers off eighteen tanks at the arsenal. They threw stones at the headlights and broke them on eight of the tanks. They took out wireless valves and broke them just to hear the bang they made. The whole instrument panel in one tank was ripped out. A box was forced open and a gun sight removed.

The damage was said to amount to the cost of £84, but this did not cover the time spent examining the tanks and repairing them. The boys were committed to the Central Criminal Court, charged with intent to impede the movement of vehicles in His Majesty's service. It seems that the eldest boy may have been seen as the ringleader as he was the only one not granted bail.

GREENWICH

Attacks on the river itself were quite common and it was not only bombs that enemy planes dropped. Just opposite Greenwich Naval College the Luftwaffe had dropped mines in the river in November 1940; when a tug and a line of barges hit a mine it vanished below the water.

The C Platoon of the 16th (Greenwich) Company Home Guard was registered in May 1940 and had an experienced drill sergeant in W. Guest. The platoon was very busy every night once the Blitz began. Bombs regularly dropped around their headquarters.

The platoon often did the work of the fire crews who were busy elsewhere, as well as guarding bombed premises. The bombs eventually scored a direct hit and the group's headquarters were destroyed on 14 November. The importance of the area as a target for the enemy was shown when the new headquarters were also damaged by bombing.

Perhaps the closest the enemy came to inflicting severe damage on the platoon was on the evening of 19 April 1941, when a bomb fell through the building and into the basement where twenty of the men were resting. The bomb failed to explode and one of the men actually stood on it as he turned off the gas. They carried on and removed the stores despite the presence of the bomb.

There were several older buildings put to a new use during the war. One of these was the dungeon underneath the Royal Naval College at Greenwich – ideal for use as air raid shelters. The dungeon had been fitted with hammocks and armchairs so that the naval ratings using the shelters would have some level of comfort.

The dungeons had air conditioning and electric lights. There was also a first-aid area. There were still pipes in place that had carried water from Greenwich Park to Greenwich Palace in the fifteenth century. The previous royal occupants of the area, such as Henry VIII, would have had little idea of what use their old dungeons would be put to.

It seems that the dungeons were not the only underground places in the area. A letter in *The Times* on 31 August 1939 claimed that there were numerous tunnels under Greenwich Park and Blackheath, many large enough for a man on horseback to ride through. There were openings to these by the Ursuline Convent and in old gravel pits.

Some of the tunnels were supposedly water conduits, but another was alleged to lead to an old Tudor mansion at Charlton. Subsidence in the road at an old house in Crooms Hill was also thought to have been because of the collapse of an old tunnel.

Deptford

During the fifth column scares of 1939/40, one of the supposed targets of these groups was thought to be Deptford. There were plans to organise a group of trustworthy citizens who would be armed to guard the important places such as the ARP control room. Even during the war, however, private armed groups were frowned upon and the group never came into being.

Luckily, before the group was organised, the local defence volunteers, the Home Guard, were formed. A company of the 25th Battalion London Home Guard was the only company enrolled by the mayor. The company would often parade through the streets with borrowed rifles. No one watching the parades was aware that the rifles did not work.

There would seem to be reasons for having a strong guard on the works in the area, as in October 1939 a man was imprisoned for striking a sentry. A labourer from Deptford was sentenced to three months in prison. It seems that he approached the sentry and claimed to work in the depot that the soldier was guarding. The sentry refused to let him in as he had been given orders that only officers were allowed to enter. The man then struck the sentry. When sentencing the attacker, the magistrate told him that he could well have been shot or bayoneted.

London

In 1932, the Tower, the oldest defensive building in the city, was used to house a prisoner for the first time in many years – Lieutenant Norman Baillie-Stewart had been caught selling secrets to the Germans.

In May 1939 there was a rehearsal for Empire Air Day on the 20th when a number of warplanes flew over London. This included a squadron of Spitfires,

The RAF memorial which stands on the Embankment near Westminster Bridge.

The Merchant Navy Memorial at Tower Hill. It contains the names of those who died at sea in the Second World War.

HMS *Belfast* was in service throughout the Second World War and took part in the Normandy landings. It is now moored at Tower Hill and is open to the public.

six squadrons of Hurricanes and two formations of Bristol Blenheims and Fairey Battles. This was also no doubt an opportunity to display the air power that the country possessed, which was in fact not as powerful as the display may have made the population think.

One of the heaviest air attacks of the war took place on 7 September 1940 when 300 German bombers attacked the docks accompanied by around 600 fighter planes. The large number of fires the bombing started could be seen 10 miles away. The light from the fires also helped to guide in more enemy bombers.

London had what was perhaps the most exclusive Home Guard unit in the country. The 2nd City of London (Civil Service) Battalion contained members from numerous government departments. Its fellows included diplomats and high-ranking naval, air force and military officers from the First World War. Their duties included guarding important buildings and bridges.

The battalion were often used as a guard of honour for several important people, including royalty. It should not be thought, however, that they were a purely ceremonial unit. Two of the battalion died in autumn 1940 while on duty in the Blitz and another member was killed near his home while trying to save people trapped in a bombed house.

RICHMOND

When evacuation areas were decided in January 1939, there were to be three distinct classifications. These were Evacuation Areas, from which evacuation would take place; Neutral Areas, where no evacuation would take place but would receive no evacuees; and Reception Areas where evacuees would go. Richmond was classed as a Neutral Area.

Richmond presents a very peaceful scene overlooking the river, but things were not quite so serene during the war.

Richmond took part in a large scale blackout practice on 9 August 1939. While the blackout was in operation, RAF planes flew over areas involved to check its success. When evacuation began on 1 September 1939, Richmond played its part when trains from the railway station were used to take evacuees away to safety. Many stations were actually closed to the public while children were being loaded on special trains. Some services were restricted in wartime and several bus routes were cancelled when war began, including the 207 route from Richmond Park to Barnes. The cancelled routes were covered by other means of transport, such as trains.

A number of open spaces were also closed to the public during the conflict, including Kew Gardens, which was closed in early September 1939. The reason given was lack of air raid shelters for visitors. It was, however, reopened three weeks later. Richmond Park was also closed to the public for a time, but had partly reopened by August 1941.

The park also played another part in the war when it was used for allotments. Part of the park that was at first chosen for this use, near Bog Gate East Sheen, was later decided to be unsuitable. Barnes Council did not agree and took advice from an expert who said that the land would be suitable for growing potatoes and vegetables.

The Richmond Home Guard had very close connections with the River Thames. The 63rd Surrey (Richmond) Battalion V Zone Home Guard was at first used to guard the bridges across the river in their area. They also had to guard Kew Observatory.

Their observation post on top of Richmond Hill was a stiff climb for some of the older members. This included some very distinguished men, including Major C.W. Cowell, who had been a member of Lord Allenby's staff in the First World War.

There were several bombs that fell on the area, including one heavy raid when Richmond seemed to be the target of the bombers. One of these bombs was very large and made an enormous crater that broke a water main. One man fell into the crater and had to swim to get out.

TEDDINGTON

One group of volunteers that was formed before the local defence volunteers came into being was the Upper Thames Patrol. The patrol operated on the non-tidal Thames between Teddington and Lechlade, a distance of 125 miles. It later became part of the local defence volunteers.

Owners of motor launches put themselves and their boats at the disposal of the patrol. One of the members of the Upper Thames Patrol was well known for other reasons. Harry Gordon-Roberts was a goalkeeper for Oxford City reserves. He was later to become the Mayor of Oxford in 1958.

The patrol had very close working relationships with the other army, RAF and Home Guard units in the areas along the Thames. The patrol was responsible for saving many people from drowning. They also helped out with buildings along the river that were bombed.

In keeping with other small boats, a number of them went across to Dunkirk. These were *The Constant Nymph* with Corporal B.A. Smith, *Surrey* with Corporal E.T. Thomas and *Bobell* with Private A.B. Cox.

The Upper Thames Patrol were a waterborne form of the Home Guard.

KINGSTON

Kingston was the site of a large barracks, which had been in existence since the nineteenth century. A man from the barracks who was a member of the East Surrey Regiment found himself in trouble in August 1939. He had appeared at the South Western Police Court where he was charged with desertion. He was handed over to a military escort but escaped after leaving Kingston railway station on his way to the barracks. The escort actually chased him on bicycles but he got away.

WINDSOR

The towns along the Thames mostly had their own Home Guard units, apart from the unit that worked on launches on the river. In Windsor, the volunteers enrolled at the police station that was then in St Leonard's Road. The upper age limit was sixty-five but there were certainly many who were economical with the truth concerning their age and it is thought that most Home Guard units may have had some Boer War veterans as members. There were certainly many First World War veterans.

Training of the unit took place at St Katherine's Hall in Clarence Road. The patrols at night, however, used to be based at Vale House Stables. Training would often include the making of petrol bombs, especially before there were any decent weapons available.

In Windsor the commanding officer of the Home Guard was Sir George Crichton, who served in the Boer War and the First World War. He was later succeeded by Colonel Reid.

The early days of the Home Guard was spent building barricades. Bags of earth were used in place of sand bags. These barricades were supposed to stop the Germans in the event of an invasion. There was very little cooperation between different units in the early days and this often led to ridiculous situations. While the Windsor barricades were placed to prevent an invasion coming from Bray, the Bray barricades were built to stop the invasion coming from Windsor.

Outdoor training took place at several open spaces such as the racecourse, the Great Park and the playing field at the Imperial Service College. There was also a rifle range in the Great Park.

In June 1941 the king was in Windsor, along with the queen and the princesses Elizabeth and Margaret, to take the salute at a services parade to mark the town's War Weapons Week, which raised £712,356. The parade was over a mile in length and included participants as diverse as the Grenadier Guards, the Navy, a Canadian RAF unit, the Home Guard and Boy Scouts. The procession was in the Grand Quadrangle of the castle and ended at the Household Cavalry barracks.

MAIDENHEAD

There was a serious misuse of rations in the town in April 1943 and the stiff sentences meted out showed how serious rationing offences were dealt with during the war. Charles Lurie, director of the Maidenhead firm, Gringershill, and his father Joseph Lurie, a director of Klein and Lurie of Middleton-on-Sea, were charged with the disposal of 3,000,000 eggs.

The men pleaded guilty to conspiring together along with another man, Horace Rayner, to furnishing false documents to the Ministry of Food with intent to deceive. In November 1940, Klein and Lurie were appointed to be a distribution firm. They were allocated more eggs than they should have been and provided false returns to cover the disposal of them.

The actual numbers involved make it hard imagine how such an event could have happened. Joseph Lurie was sentenced to three years' imprisonment and a fine of £2,000, while his son was sentenced to six months. Rayner was fined £25.

The arrival of thousands of Americans in the country in 1942 was greeted with mixed emotions by the population. Although the majority were pleased to welcome their new allies, some men had misgivings, often due to the impression that the well-off Americans had on the female population of the country.

In August 1942, an American club for Air Transport auxiliary pilots was opened. The opening was marked with a speech by Sir Edward Grigg, chairman of a committee appointed to help open such centres as a welcome to the Americans. He described the cooperation between two great nations as vital to the civilised world.

Sir Edward also mentioned how his committee had received so many offers of help and offers from people from all walks of life to put up Americans in their own homes. He also acknowledged that there were stories suggesting that such a spirit of welcome did not exist. These stories were to be found in so many different places that they could not, he claimed, have been started by accident. Those who repeated the rumours were, he claimed, playing into the hands of Dr Goebbels.

After the war, the men of Maidenhead returning from the conflict were greeted with a letter from the mayor. It was to congratulate them on their release from active service and stated that they had not been forgotten during their absence. They would, it was hoped, be able to settle back down into civil life. The letter reminded the men that if they had any problems that the Citizens' Advice Bureau at the Town Hall had a panel of experts at its disposal ready to help.

With the letter came an award of a medallion of Field Marshal Montgomery, who had been awarded the freedom of the borough as a tribute to him and all the British Armed Forces who took part in service during the war.

READING

There was a unit of the Pioneer Corps based in Reading during the war and they supported the local Home Guard. They performed guard duty and took part in weekend camps on the Downs. In one of these camps, at Arborfield, the Pioneers and the Home Guard were trained to search woodland for German parachutists.

After bomb damage to the Supermarine works at Southampton, Spitfire production was moved to other parts of the country. Many of the aircraft components were made in Reading. The parts were then taken to Henley Airfield near Wargrave. There was also an aircraft called the Henley. The Hawker Henley was originally meant to be a light bomber but then it was changed to a target tug. It was found to be unsuitable for this, however, as the engine often cut out, leading to the loss of several planes.

It is interesting to see the Russian flag flying along with the British and American flags at this gathering of the RAF Technical Training Command at Wantage Hall, Reading, in 1945.

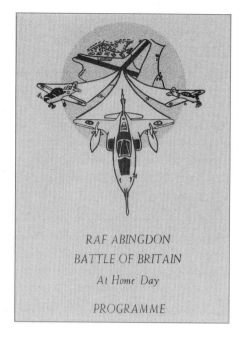

RAF ABINGDON

BATTLE OF BRITAIN

At Home Day

PROGRAMME

Above: A badge from RAF Abingdon.
Left: RAF Abingdon was responsible for several open days and flying displays as this programme from the 1970s shows.

ABINGDON

Abingdon was the site of an RAF airfield during the war. The airfield actually opened in 1932 and, until the outbreak of the war, was home to two bomber squadrons. Once the war began, the field was used to train bomber crews; Wellingtons and Whitleys from the base also took part in raids over Germany.

After the war, Dakotas were based at Abingdon and were used for transport. It was from Abingdon that the first aircraft to be involved in the Berlin Airlift of in July 1948 took off. The field then became a ferrying base used to fly aircraft overseas.

Since the early 1980s, RAF Abingdon has been used as a repair and salvage base. Many of the aircraft used in displays are based there. It is also used to train university graduates interested in joining the RAF to fly. In the 1990s it was given to the army and is now known as Dalton Barracks.

OXFORD

Oxford had an unusual Home Guard unit in comparison with others. The Oxford University Senior Training Corps was very different to the normal Home Guard unit. They were already guarding important sites while the local defence volunteers were being formed, although they later became part of the Home Guard. They also provided a mobile column.

There was also another group, the 6th Oxfordshire (Oxford City) Battalion Home Guard. It was formed in May 1940 and had over 1,200 members. They were the first Home Guard unit to have an artillery section and were given access to the guns of the Oxford Senior Training Corps.

The university played a different part in the war effort in October 1940 when there was a call for metal from iron railings. The permission for use of railings on private property had to be given by the owner. The bursar of St John's College, which owned a great deal of property in the town, gave permission for the removal of railings which led to 400 tons of metal being collected.

The area also played another important role in the war. By the summer of 1940, the public were banned from visiting many of the seaside resorts that they had once gone to for holidays. There was one place that they could still find peace and quiet to help them relax and forget the stress of nightly air raids. The upper Thames was the ideal place to spend the short periods of leisure time that the men women and often children of the country had off from working for the war effort.

The steamers that travelled between Oxford and Kingston were full, despite the war. Campsites along the river were also full. The conflict had an effect on the river, however, as many of the Thames lock-keepers were naval reservists who had gone off to war, leaving the work to be done by women and children. The crew of the steamers also did their bit and often wore Home Guard armbands while carrying the loads of pleasure seekers.

Oxford had close connections with the war in the air during the Second World War. There was an aircraft that although built in Portsmouth by De Havilland, was called the Airspeed Oxford. It was a military version of the Airspeed Envoy and was used to train bomber crews.

The Oxford area had a more than its fair share of airfields during the war. RAF Chalgrove was used by the RAF and the 8th and 9th United States Army Air Force. It was also known at one point as USAAF Airfield 465. There was also Mount Farm and RAF Benson, which stayed in RAF hands throughout the war.

RAF Chalgrove was built to accommodate aeroplanes up to the size of bombers. The land was given to the Americans in November 1942 and the airfield was constructed by McAlpine. There were three runways and hard standing for fifty aircraft. The site also included accommodation for over 2,000 personnel.

The Airspeed Oxford was used as a training aeroplane for bomber crews during the war.

The airfield was originally occupied by the 10th Reconnaissance Group in January 1944. The group was mainly provided with the P-51 Mustang and the P-38 Lightning. They were responsible for photographing targets and for assessing bomb damage after raids. They were responsible for recording much of the coastal area used to land allied forces on D-Day.

At one time Mount Farm had a famous commanding officer. Colonel Elliot Roosevelt, son of F.D. Roosevelt, took over the farmhouse as his quarters, evicting the pilots who had been using it. No doubt his father's influence helped.

The airfield was returned to the RAF in 1946 and, for a short period, was used to train photo-reconnaissance pilots.

During the war, Vera Lynn came to Benson to entertain the personnel based there. It was then closed a few months later and was leased to Martin-Baker in 1946 and is still in use as a private airfield today.

RAF Benson was another airfield in the region of Oxford that opened in 1939. It was the home to the No. 1 Photographic Reconnaissance Unit. They stayed at the base for most of the war. One of the jobs they carried out was to record the damage done by the famous Dambusters flight. In 1946, the King's Flight was based there and stayed until 1995.

The base is now the home of Puma helicopters of 33 Squadron, Merlin HC3 helicopters of 28 (AC) Squadron and the tutor T1 aircraft of the Oxford University Air Squadron.

The presence of so many airfields in the area may not have had the protective effect that one would have thought. A speech by Air Chief Marshall Sir Robert Brooke-Popham during the war explained how air superiority was often temporary. There was no local defence by aircraft and enemy planes attacking Oxford could be brought down in Sussex by a squadron of fighters from Kent.

CRICKLADE

There was a very unusual event concerning Cricklade in March 1943. It involved Major General Sir Percy Robert Lawrie, Provost Marshal of England and former Assistant Commissioner of the Metropolitan Police. His address was given as Hyde Park Gate, but he also had an address at the Manor House, Cricklade.

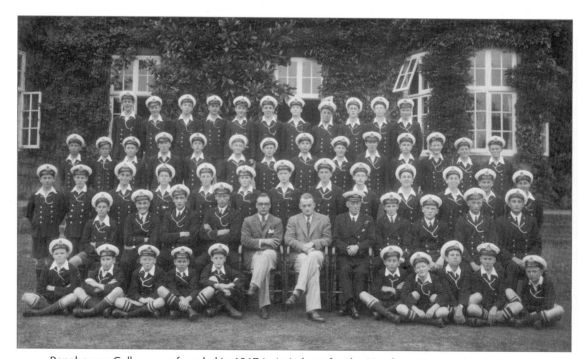

Pangbourne College was founded in 1917 to train boys for the Merchant Navy. It then began to train them for the Royal Navy. This photograph dates from the 1930s.

Sir Percy was summoned to Bow Street Court for making a false statement to obtain a new ration book, for unlawfully using the book and for failing to deliver it to the Ministry for Food. He pleaded not guilty. The application for the new book was made in Cricklade and he had described himself as a retired army officer.

Sir Percy had in fact been re-employed by the army in 1940 and became Provost Marshal in charge of military police in July that year. Sir Percy explained that he thought he should use the book when he was at home and his army ration book when he was travelling. There were occasions, however, when both books were used. Sir Percy was fined £550.

CIRENCESTER

Plans for evacuation were drawn up well before the war began when areas were designated as Reception, Evacuation or Neutral Areas. In March 1939, a proposal was put forward by Cirencester District Council to the local MP Mr W.S. Morrison.

It was proposed that evacuation areas should be adopted by a reception area. The idea that certain houses should be exempt from the billeting of evacuees was put forward by Captain F.B. Swanwick. This would include cases of hardship and those undertaking important war work. Billeting would also be supplemented by camps erected by local authorities. The camps would take children and mothers who would then help look after them. The camps would have also been used to house those who were bombed out. The idea does not seem to have been taken up, despite the advantages that it seemed to offer.

Cirencester was the site of RAF Kemble and the building of the airfield was started in 1936. It was occupied by No. 5 Maintenance Unit and by the end of 1939 there were over 600 aircraft on the site, mainly Hurricanes. Planes were sent there from the factories and then sent on to their units.

In May 1939, there was a display of Britain's air power, although it was not as strong as was needed to face what was to come. There was a parade of warplanes over London and another over the West of England. This included a flight of seventy-two Fairey Battle bombers. Although essentially a practice for Empire Air Day, it must have been seen by the public as a display of air power. The bombers assembled in the Abingdon area and then flew over Cirencester and on to the West Country.

From 1940, aircraft were prepared at Kemble for longer flights overseas. This was known as the Overseas Aircraft Preparation Unit. Kemble prepared over 2,000 aircraft in 1941. During the following two years, the base was extended and the runways lengthened.

During the 1950s, the airfield began to take delivery of jet aircraft. This continued along with the Red Arrows, who were based there during the 1960s until the base was given over to the Americans. After the Americans left, the airfield closed in 1992. It was later to come to life again, being used by flying clubs and as a base for scrapping old aircraft. There are also annual flying displays at the site.

Bibliography

BOOKS

Anderson, J., *Anchor and Hope*, Hodder & Stoughton, 1980
Armstrong, W., *The Thames from its Rise to the Nore*, J.S. Virtue & Co, ND
Astbury, A., *Estuary*, The Carnforth Press, 1980
Bevan, B., *Edward III, Monarch of Chivalry*, Rubicon, 1992
Bloomfield, P., *Kent and the Napoleonic Wars*, Alan Sutton Publishing, 1987
Bryant, A. *Liquid History*, privately printed, 1960
Collingwood, R., *The Archaeology of Roman Britain*, Bracken Books, 1996
Cruickshank, D., *Invasion*, Boxtree, 2001
Defoe, D., *A Tour Through The Eastern Counties*, Cassell's National Library, 1722
Foley, M., *Front Line Kent*, Sutton Publishing, 2006
——, *Hard As Nails*, Spellmount, 2007
Gibbings, R., *Sweet Thames Run Softly*, J. Dent & Sons, 1940
Grainge, G., *The Roman Invasions of Britain*, Tempus Publishing, 2005
Graves, C., *The Home Guard Of Britain*, Hutchinson & Co., 1943
Gulvin, K.R., *The Medway Forts*, The Fort Amherst and Lines Trust, 2000
Harvey, W., *Whitstable and the French Prisoners of War*, Wallace Harvey, 1971
Hassall, T.G., *Oxford Castle*, T.G. Hassall, 1971
Hill, C., *The Century of Revolution*, Van Nostran Reinhold, 1987
Howson, J., *A Brief History of Barking and Dagenham*, London Borough of Barking and Dagenham, 1965
Jenkins, A., *The Thames*, Macmillan, 1983
Kemble, J., *Prehistoric & Roman Essex*, Tempus Publishing, 2001
Kerrigan, C., *A History of Tower Hamlets*, London Borough of Tower Hamlets, 1982
Marcus, G., *A Naval History of England*, Longmans, 1961
Morgan, G., *Forgotten Thameside*, Thames Bank Publishing Co., 1951
Salter's Guide to the Thames, 34th edition, 1932
Stephens, W., *The Thames*, Muller, Blond & White, 1986
Strugnell, K., *Seagates to the Saxon Shore*, Terence Dalton, 1973
Tames, R., *Barking Past*, Historical Publications, 2002
Thompson, L., *The Land that Fans The Thames*, Tindal Press, 1957
Trease, S., *Samuel Pepys And His World*, Thames & Hudson, 1972
Turner, F., *The Maunsell Sea Forts*, Turner, 1997
——, *The Wreck of the USS Richard Montgomery*, Turner, 1995

Weightman, G., *London River*, Collins & Brown, 1990

Wessels, A., *Lord Kitchener and the War in South Africa*, Army Records Society, 2006

White, A., *Tideways and Byways in Essex and Suffolk*, Edward Arnold, 1948

ARTICLES, DOCUMENTS & NEWSPAPERS

A Company's Story in its Setting, Samuel Williams & Co., 1955

Burrows, J., 'Tilbury Fort', Journal of the British Archaeological Association, 38 (1), 1932

English Illustrated Magazine, 1890–1

Essex Record Office Documents: D/Deb 95/20, T/P 110/50, T/A 235/1

Greenwood, P., 'Uphall Camp, An Iron Age Fortification', *London Archaeologist*, Autumn, 1989

Illustrated London News: 6 January 1849, 15 July 1854, 22 July 1854, 7 October 1854

Penny Magazine, 1841

Powell, W., 'The Medieval Hospitals at East and West Tilbury and Henry VIII's Forts', *Essex Archaeology & History*, 19, 1988

Royal Commission on Historical Monuments – Essex, (South East), 1923

Saunders, A., 'Tilbury Fort and the Development of Artillery Fortifications in the Thames Estuary', *Antiquaries Journal*, 40, London, 1960

The Times, 2 June 1797, 18 August 1797, 23 August 1856, 1 February 1877, 5 April 1877, 6 September 1914, 27 November 1914, 12 May 1917

The War & Thames Board Mills, Thames Board Mills

Index